Francis
and
Clare

A Gospel Story

S0-BZW-173

Francis and Clare

A Gospel Story

Helen Julian, CSF

the WORD among us®

Copyright 2001 by © Helen Julian, CSF
All rights reserved
ISBN: 1-59325-060-6

Originally published under the title *Living the Gospel:
The Spirituality of St. Francis and St. Clare* in 2001 by The Bible Reading
Fellowship, Oxford, U.K.

Published in 2005 by The Word Among Us Press
9639 Doctor Perry Road
Ijamsville, Maryland 21754
www.wordamongus.org

10 09 08 07 06 05   1 2 3 4 5 6

Cover design by Evelyn Harris
Giotto di Bondone (1266-1336) Story of Saint Francis of Assisi: Saint Francis,
Saint Clare, Saint Vittorino and Saint Rufino. S. Francesco, Assisi, Italy
Photo Credit: Scala / Art Resource, NY

Scripture quotations are taken from The New Revised Standard Version
of the Bible, copyright © 1989, 1995 by the Division of Christian Education of the
National Council of the Churches of Christ in the USA,
and are used by permission. All rights reserved.

Excerpts from *Frances and Clare: The Complete Works*, from The Classics of
Western Spirituality, translated by Regis J. Armstrong, O.F.M. CAP, and Ignatius C.
Brady, O.F.M., Copyright © 1982 by Paulist Press, Inc., New York/Mahwah, N.J.
Used with permission of Paulist Press: www.paulistpress.com

Excerpts from *The Daily Office SSF* are copyright ©
The Society of St. Francis, 1992.

No part of this publication may be reproduced, stored in a retrieval system, or
transmitted in any form or by any means—electronic, mechanical, photocopy,
recording, or any other—except for brief quotations in printed reviews, without the
prior permission of the publisher.

Made and printed in the United States of America

Library of Congress Cataloging-in-Publication Data

Julian, Helen.
  Francis and Clare : a gospel story / Helen Julian.-- 1st American pbk. ed.
    p. cm.
  Originally published: Living the Gospel. Oxford : Bible Reading
Fellowship, 2001.
  Includes bibliographical references.
  ISBN 1-59325-060-6 (alk. paper)
  1. Francis, of Assisi, Saint, 1182-1226. 2. Clare, of Assisi, Saint,
1194-1253. I. Title.
  BX4700.F6J78 2005
  271'.302--dc22

                              2005013195

Contents

Chapter 1

Roots

February 1208. A young Italian goes to Mass in the little church of St. Mary of the Angels, on the plain below the Umbrian town of Assisi. It is the feast day of St. Matthias, and the gospel reading is of Jesus sending out his disciples: "As you go, proclaim the good news, 'The kingdom of heaven has come near.' Take no gold, or silver, or copper in your belts, no bag for your journey, or two tunics, or sandals, or a staff. . . ." (Matthew 10:7, 9-10).

Hearing these words, the young man is filled with joy. "This is what I want," he cries out. "This is what I long for with all my heart."[1] And immediately he begins to put into practice what he has heard. He takes off his shoes, lays aside his staff, keeps only one tunic, replaces his belt and purse with a length of rope. It is the latest and perhaps the most definitive turning point in the life of Francesco Bernardone. And it is one that in its immediate response to a word from God, and its desire to live the gospel literally, is very characteristic of the man who will become known as St. Francis of Assisi.

In 1208 Francis was twenty-six years old, and this was the latest of a series of encounters with God that had gradually drawn him away from his life as the rich and spoiled son of an Assisi cloth merchant. His response to the gospel was in many ways new and fresh, reflecting the rapidly changing times in which he lived.

Francis' early life as the son of Pietro Bernardone, a successful merchant, and his wife, Pica, is in itself characteristic of the changing society of his times. He was born in the golden age of the merchants, and cloth merchants were foremost among those who were trading throughout Europe. Francis was baptized Giovanni (John) but was soon nicknamed Francesco, "the little Frenchman," because of his father's close trading links with that country.

The merchants settled in groups in places advantageous for their trade—near a port, or at a crossroads on the new network of roads that was springing up. Thus new towns and cities came into being, and old ones were revived, shifting the balance of both population and power from rural to urban areas. Initially the cities were still subject to the local feudal lord—an abbot, bishop, or count—and their inhabitants still had to fulfill the obligations of the feudal system. The lord exacted taxes and tolls, gave permission to travel, settled disputes, and meted out justice.

But this system was changing. In the towns, tradesmen, craftsmen, and merchants banded together into associations, or communes, which sought freedom, politically and economically, from the feudal overlords. This brought about not only the political and economic changes they sought, but also a major change in human relationships and in the way society worked. Feudal society was hierarchical, based on a vertical relationship between an inferior and a superior, which bound each person to the one over them. The new society of the urban centers was based on horizontal relationships, freely entered into, which bound each person to the group.

The model relationship was that of brother, not of master and servant, overlord and vassal. Francis reflected this new ideal when he named the community he founded the Little or Lesser Brothers—in Latin, the Fratres Minores.

As the feudal system broke down, the balance of power in society shifted. Francis, as a merchant's son, was part of the newly prosperous urban class who were challenging the power of the traditional rural ruling classes, represented by the bishop and the lord of the manor. Of course inequality did not go away; in some ways it became more marked. But it was now based not on the accident of birth but on wealth in the form of land, possessions, and increasingly, money. In the cities, centers of consumption and trade, people began more and more to use coins: first of silver, and then of gold. Money increasingly replaced barter as the measure of value and the means of trade.

Politically, life was turbulent. Change did not happen without conflict and difficulty. In Assisi, as in most of the growing Italian cities, there was in-fighting between the emerging middle class and the landowners, who were the traditional feudal holders of power. There were sporadic outbreaks of fighting with neighboring cities. And always in the background were the tensions between the Emperor Frederick II of the Holy Roman Empire and successive popes. On the world stage, Christians and Muslims fought over the Holy Land, with the Third Crusade launched in 1193, and the Fourth Crusade in 1202.

The church too was in a period of change. The turning of the first millennium in 1000 had sparked off a process of reform, fueled by a desire to return to the sources of the faith. First worked out in the Gregorian reform of the reign of Pope

Gregory VII (1073–1085), this continued with the four Lateran Councils of 1123, 1139, 1179, and 1215—the first general councils of the church for some centuries. Their reforms were wide ranging. They sought to free the church from the domination of lay feudal power, so that bishops and abbots were elected by the church and not by the feudal overlords. Clerical celibacy was imposed at the beginning of the eleventh century. Peace-making initiatives were another expression of the zeal for reform.

The Fourth Lateran Council, convened in 1215 by Pope Innocent III, had a particular influence on Francis, coming as it did in the early days of his community. It gathered together in Rome 412 bishops and more than eight hundred abbots, priors, and other heads of religious orders. Their chief concern was to respond to the growing power of Islam, especially in the Holy Land, and to the spread of heresy. They agreed on seventy decrees covering most areas of church life—the life of the clergy, the sacraments, religious life, and the work of mission.

The influence of these decrees can be seen in a number of the writings of Francis, as can the Pope's call to priests and religious to adopt the tau (a T-shape cross), as their logo. Tau, the last letter of the Hebrew alphabet, is also the Hebrew word for "mark." From Ezekiel's vision (9:4), in which he is ordered to "put a mark" on the forehead of the redeemed, the tau became a symbol of salvation, and is used as such by John in Revelation 7:3-4 and 22:4. Francis signed all his letters with it, and it has become the characteristically Franciscan form of the cross.

Part of the change in the church was the establishment of new or reformed religious orders. The Carthusians and the Cistercians sought a return to the simplicity of the original Bene-dictine rule and a better balance between manual work and prayer. The canonical movement—groups of priests living in community, particularly those following an Augustinian rule—also moved to a new balance between active and contemplative life. Increasingly they chose to live in the growing towns, and combined community life with parish work. In all these new or reformed male orders, the lay brothers, those not ordained to the priesthood, played an increasing role. And outside the orders, old or new, more and more lay people sought a life in community, but not confined by traditional models of religious life or bound by the existing rules.

One of the main manifestations of this desire among women centered on the Low Countries. Groups of women came together spontaneously to live lives of poverty, chastity, and ser-vice to others, but without taking formal vows. They became known as Beguines. They lived modestly, in their own homes or in groups, valuing manual work and serving the poor, often in schools or hospitals that they founded and ran. They also preached and wrote, and this brought them into conflict with the church.

The church was anxious about these developments, and dealt badly with several groups, treating them as heretical when in fact they were not. One group that suffered in this way was the Waldensians.

The Waldensians were poor people of the French city of Lyons who, around 1170, in response to the preaching of a merchant, Peter Waldo, began to devote their lives to prayer and good works, reading the Bible, preaching, and begging.

They spread rapidly; trade and urbanization allowed not only money and goods but also ideas to circulate widely. Preaching played an important part in this spread of ideas. But in the medieval church, permission to preach was given by the bishops, the successors of the apostles—and only to priests. No lay man, nor any woman, could claim this right. In 1184 Pope Lucius III excommunicated not only the Cathars, a genuinely heretical group, but also the Waldensians.

The turning points in Francis' life happened in this context. His early years, as the favorite son of Pietro and Pica Bernardone, were spent in relative luxury. He was popular, a leader among the young men of Assisi, charming, witty, and generous. Although the only pictures we have of him were painted after his death, we do have a verbal portrait, written by his first biographer, Thomas of Celano. Thomas joined the Franciscan order while Francis was still alive, so it is reasonable to assume that he writes here from personal knowledge. Francis, he says, was quite short, with black eyes, hair, and beard; he had a long face, with a straight nose and small, upright ears. His arms were short, but his hands and fingers were slender and long. His voice was "strong, sweet, clear, and sonorous."[2]

The first setback in Francis' life came at the age of twenty, when, full of the romantic ideals of knighthood and chivalry, he rode off to battle against the neighboring city of Perugia. Perugia won this battle, and Francis, along with many others from Assisi, was taken prisoner. A year's imprisonment (ending when illness enabled his father to ransom him) and then a year's convalescence left Francis disconsolate and unsettled. For a time he worked in his father's business again. But it was out of this time of difficulty and disappointment that he began to get an inkling of what God wanted of him.

The first voice came in a dream. Francis, making another attempt to be a knight, was in Spoleto (a town about twenty-two miles south of Assisi). In his dream he saw a castle, with a large room covered in shields, all of them belonging to Francis and his followers. His first understanding of the dream was mistaken—and he eagerly embraced what he saw as a prophecy of successful knighthood leading to glory. Then a voice asked him, "Francis, is it better to serve the Lord or the servant?"

"The Lord, of course."

"Then why are you trying to turn your Lord into a servant?"

Francis recognized God's voice and, like the boy Samuel in the temple, responded, "Lord, what do you want me to do?"

And the voice asked a hard thing. "Return to Assisi. There you will be shown what to do and come to understand this vision."

So Francis returned to Assisi, a humiliating turnaround. To his friends he would seem a knight who had fled the battlefield, the ultimate shame in chivalry. Francis spent the whole of the next year praying in a cave outside Assisi, living as a hermit, trying to come to terms with what God might be asking of him. It was not an easy or instant conversion, and he was not immediately given a blueprint for his whole future. God unfolded his plan for Francis one piece at a time.

The next encounter is the one that Francis himself always identified as the beginning of his conversion. On a road on the plain below Assisi, he saw a leper in the distance. He had always had a great fear of sufferers from this contagious disease and had gone out of his way to avoid them. Celano tells us that Francis would only look at their houses from a safe distance of two miles, holding his nose with his hands. But now he was given the courage not only to remain on the road, not only to give the leper alms, but to embrace him. In some versions of the story, the leper then vanished. Was he in fact Christ, coming to Francis in the form of the most needy and most despised? Whatever actually happened, it was a crucial turning point for Francis—his first moment of reaching out, of finding God in the poor, and somehow being enabled to overcome his fears. For a time he went to live with the lepers, serving them and bringing the good news of the gospel to them.

During this period he continued to spend much time in prayer, often in remote and semi-derelict churches. One of these was the small church of San Damiano, not far outside Assisi. While praying there one day in 1206, he seemed to hear the figure on the crucifix over the altar speak to him. "Francis," it said, "go and rebuild my church, which as you see is falling down." It was the next piece of the jigsaw, and Francis as ever responded immediately and enthusiastically. He began to collect stones and to rebuild San Damiano. When he ran out of money, he took some cloth from his father's shop, sold it, and offered the money to the priest at San Damiano, who prudently refused to accept it.

It was the final straw for his father. He dragged Francis to the bishop's palace, and there, in front of the bishop and a crowd of curious onlookers, demanded that Francis renounce all his rights as his son, and return everything he had been given by his father. In a moment of dramatic symbolism, Francis stripped off his clothes and laid them at the feet of the bishop. "From now on," he said, "I will not call Pietro Bernardone my father, but only God, my Father in heaven." It was the final renunciation of his old life, and a rift with his father that seems never to have been repaired. The bishop, the representative of the church, covered Francis with his cloak, and perhaps in this we can see the change of allegiance acted out. There was now no turning back for Francis.

In order to continue his work of rebuilding churches, he took to begging on the streets of Assisi. Many of the people thought he was mad and threw stones at him. Wandering through the woods one day, he was attacked by robbers and beaten up. For a time he worked as a kitchen hand at a nearby monastery, but was so badly treated that he was forced to leave. But despite these difficulties, Francis continued to follow God's call. When San Damiano had been repaired, he moved on to rebuild other churches, and it was while working on Santa Maria degli Angeli that he went to Mass on St. Matthias' Day and heard the gospel reading that shaped the rest of his life.

In obedience to the message he had heard, "Proclaim the good news" (Matthew 10:7), Francis now began to preach. Many mocked him, but some were intrigued and challenged by what he said. Within a year, first in ones and twos, then very rapidly in larger numbers, men came to join him. He had not begun with any intention of founding a community, but very soon he found that he had one anyway. He saw this always as God's work. In his Testament, written near the end of his life, he wrote, "After the Lord gave me brothers. . . ."[3]

While the first men were joining Francis in what would become a community of brothers, a woman was also listening to him preach and hearing through his words God's call to her. Chiara (Clare) Favarone, who in 1210 was sixteen years old, twelve years younger than Francis, belonged to the other power group in the city—the nobility. Her family spent much time in exile from Assisi during Clare's childhood, including two years in Perugia, while Francis was fighting on the other side of this particular conflict. Clare's father, Lord Favarone, was a powerful noble, and her mother, Ortolana, a pious woman who loved to go on pilgrimages. The year before Clare's birth, she had traveled as far as the Holy Land. The family lived in a grand house on the piazza near the cathedral of San Rufino, in the heart of Assisi.

Clare, the third of five children and the eldest daughter of the family, seems to have been marked out for holiness from an early age, unlike Francis. When Ortolana was pregnant with Clare, she was praying one day before the cross, asking God to help her in the dangers of childbirth. Then she heard a voice reassuring her and telling her that she would give birth to a light that would wonderfully light up the world. When her daughter was born, she named her Chiara, which means "light."

Clare was a serious child, and from an early age she cared for the poor and needy. She put aside the food she was given and sent it to the poor. She refused many offers of marriage to prestigious and wealthy men. Increasingly she was captivated by the preaching of the cloth merchant's son. Despite the difficulties for a young unmarried woman of meeting any man outside her own household, she managed to meet and talk with

Francis secretly, accompanied only by a friend, Bona. Francis' vision kindled her own, and she determined to join him.

On Palm Sunday 1212 she went to the cathedral, and in what seems to have been a prearranged signal, did not go up with the rest of the congregation to receive her blessed palm. Instead the bishop came to her where she sat and gave her the palm. That night she left her parents' house secretly to join Francis. It was a brave and extraordinary thing to do, putting her beyond the pale of her class and bringing shame on her family. In some stories this is emphasized by the detail that she left by a door that was normally only opened when someone died. On the natural level, this demonstrates her determination, in opening the blocked-up door. But it contains also the symbolism of dying to her former life. And this symbolism is strengthened by her leaving at the beginning of Holy Week, as the church turned its attention to Jesus' passion, death, and resurrection.

After leaving the house, Clare was met by Francis and a few brothers. In the small chapel of the Portiuncula at St. Mary of the Angels, where the brothers had a house, she exchanged her beautiful dress for a simple habit and laid aside her jewelry. Francis himself cut her hair. She had already sold her dowry, and part of that of her sister Beatrice, and given the proceeds to the poor. Kneeling before Francis, she made a vow of obedience to him. The brothers then took her to a house of Benedictine nuns, San Paolo delle Abbadesse, one of the richest monasteries in the area.

Here Clare stayed for a few weeks, carrying out menial domestic tasks. Her family, aghast at the scandalous thing she had done, sent armed men, led by her uncle, Monaldo, the head of the family, to bring her home. For several days they tried to persuade, threaten, or force her to come home. Finally, when her parents tried to drag her out, Clare seized the altar cloth and uncovered her head, showing her shorn hair. This was a sign that her choice was irrevocable, and her uncle and his men returned home empty handed.

But worse was to follow. Sixteen days after Clare left home, her younger sister, Catherine, followed her. Clare had by now moved from San Paolo to the community of women living at Sant' Angelo in Panzo, on the slopes of Mount Subasio. Again the men came to fetch home a wayward daughter. This time they managed to lay hold of Catherine and were in fact carrying her off, when Clare prayed, and Catherine became so heavy that they could not lift her. Once again, they retired defeated.

Catherine too was received by Francis, who cut her hair and gave her the name of Agnes. The fledgling community now needed a home of its own. Francis had prophesied when rebuilding San Damiano that one day it would be the home of a community of sisters, and now he took Clare and Agnes there and established them in the first monastery of Poor Clares, so named because of their emphasis on poverty.

As men had come to join Francis, so women came to join Clare, including eventually her own mother, her youngest sister Beatrice, two of her nieces, other members of her family, and women from some of the noblest families in Assisi.

So while Francis and his brothers tramped first the roads of Italy, then other parts of Europe, and before Francis' death, also North Africa, where the first Franciscan martyrs died in Morocco, Clare and her sisters stayed in their convent in Assisi and prayed. But their hiddenness made them no less central to the Franciscan vision.

Although they saw little of each other, there was a strong relationship between Francis and Clare, and at several turning points of his life, when he was unsure of his next steps, he asked her advice. In sickness he returned to San Damiano and was cared for by Clare and the sisters. After Francis' death in 1226, Clare lived on for another twenty-seven years, and she was the most tenacious of all his followers in preserving Francis' vision—and especially his commitment to poverty—from all that threatened it.

Clare's community, too, grew beyond the confines of Assisi and of Italy. By the time of her death in 1253, there were more than 150 communities that followed her way of life. The majority were in Italy, southern France, and Spain, but they were also found as far east as Prague, and as far west as Bruges.

Both Francis and Clare sought the recognition of the church for their new communities, and both wrote Rules as part of this process, which are one of our primary sources for their vision. Given the similarity in many respects of their way of life to that of the Waldensians, recently excommunicated as heretics, it was a wise precaution.

Francis first wrote a Rule in 1209, in the early days of his brotherhood. It has not survived but is thought to have been very short and simple, less a legislative document than a vision of the gospel life. Francis himself traveled to Rome with his first brothers to present this Rule to the pope, Innocent III, and to seek the approval of the church.

The Pope listened carefully to Francis as he explained the

way of life of the brothers, and asked him to return the next day for his decision. That night Innocent III had a vivid dream. He saw the church of St. John Lateran, then the mother church of all Christendom, beginning to lean and then to topple to the ground. Just as it was about to crash down, a small beggar rushed out of the shadows and supported the church on his shoulder. Waking, the pope recognized the beggar as Francis. The next day he embraced Francis warmly and gave his approval to the new community. It was a further fulfilment of Francis' own vision at San Damiano, another sign that he was indeed called to do great things for God.

A later Rule written by Francis (rather confusingly known as the Earlier Rule) has survived, though it was never approved by the church. Approval was given to a final Rule, the Later Rule, in 1223.

Clare had somewhat more trouble in obtaining the authority of the church for the Rule she wrote. She fell foul of a decree of the Fourth Lateran Council, which had forbidden any new Rules for religious communities, and had to make do for some time with a basically Benedictine Rule, which did not provide for the intense poverty to which she was committed. She was the first woman to write a Rule for her own community, and her strength of character is demonstrated in her perseverance in seeking its approval. In fact it was only finally authorized by the pope two days before Clare's death in 1253.

While the Rules and other writings by Francis and Clare are important sources of insight into their spirituality, the stories about them are equally valuable. Neither of them wrote much—in the collected writings, just over two hundred pages contain all that is known, and this includes introductions and commentary. But each, writings and stories, can shed light on the other. In the writings we have Francis' and Clare's own voices; in the stories, the voices of those who knew them, recollections of their actions, and reflections on their lives by those who followed them.

Sometimes the writings have obviously been influenced by the need to be accepted by some official body—the Rules in particular were written in order to be authorized by the church, and compromises may have been necessary to achieve this end. The stories, on the other hand, especially those that have come down from contemporaries, give us eyewitness accounts from those who walked the roads of Italy with Francis, heard him preach, and saw him at prayer, and from those who lived with Clare at San Damiano, some of them for many years. They shed a different light, which contributes to a more rounded picture.

Of course the stories have also been influenced by their context, especially by the fact that both Francis and Clare were canonized (recognized as saints) very shortly after their deaths. The stories were inevitably increasingly influenced by official expectations of what saints were like, and by the desire of their followers to present their founders in the best possible light.

The important role of context in interpretation is not strange to readers of the Bible. The biblical narrative is always rooted in particular times and places. Unlike many of the other faiths of the ancient world that sought to transcend history—seeing time as a spiral or circle, and this world as a place from which to escape into a timeless realm—for Jews and Christians, history is sacred, and this world is the place of God's encounters with his people. God chooses a particular people, the Jews, in one small part of the ancient world, and the Bible is in its essence the story of his engagement with them, of their response or lack of it, their faithfulness or faithlessness.

Francis and Clare had a passionate response to the world around them, finding God at work in their time and place. But we do not need to be thirteenth-century Italians to learn from them or to find in them a way to draw nearer to God in our time and place. In prayer and meditation on the Bible, we can perhaps see ourselves in Adam and Eve in the garden, in Moses' encounter with God in the burning bush, in the crowd listening to Jesus on the mount, in those seeking healing from him, in the disciples meeting the risen Christ on the road to Emmaus. So as we come to know Francis and Clare, we can find ourselves listening to Francis preaching, walking the roads of Italy with the early brothers, or at prayer with Clare in San Damiano.

The different ways in which we know about Francis and Clare are echoed in the many different ways in which the Bible tells us of God. In poetry, in history, in laws, we catch different glimpses of God at work with his chosen people. But stories are at the heart of the book. Ask most people what they know of the Bible and it will be stories—Adam and Eve walking in the garden with God, David and Goliath, the children of Israel crossing the Red Sea, Noah and the ark, the stories of Jesus' life, his birth, his passion, his resurrection appearances, and the stories he told—of the good Samaritan, the prodigal son, the sower going out to sow, the merchant finding the pearl of great price. In both the Bible and in the lives of Francis and Clare, it is the stories which bring the vision to life. ❧

Chapter 2
Following Jesus

During the early days of his call, while still in Assisi, rebuilding churches and beginning to preach, Francis had quite a long period of learning and experimenting alone—and not just alone, but often mocked and despised, treated as though he were mad. The change in him from rich, beautifully dressed playboy to poor man, begging for his bread in rags, was so great that perhaps this was the only explanation his family and friends could understand.

But some looked at him with different eyes. One of these was a man called Bernard, who was one of the richest and most learned men in Assisi. Seeing how patient Francis was, and how he was not upset by ridicule or even by having stones thrown at him, Bernard was intrigued. He wanted to know more, so he invited Francis to have supper with him and to stay the night. A bed was made up for Francis in Bernard's room, and rather comically, both men pretended to be deeply asleep. Francis did not want anyone to see him at prayer; Bernard was determined to find out how Francis could so cheerfully withstand so much opposition. Francis was taken in by Bernard's loud snores, got up from his bed, and began to pray. He was so caught up in his contemplation of God's goodness that all he could say was, "My God and my all." He prayed like this all night.

In the morning, Bernard, deeply moved by what he had seen and heard, announced that he wanted to join Francis in giving up all he possessed and serving God. Francis was overjoyed inside but insisted that such an important decision should not be made hastily. He went with Bernard to the bishop's house, where they heard Mass and spent some time in prayer together. Then they asked the priest to open the missal three times and to read what he found.

The first time, he read Jesus' words to the rich young man, "If you wish to be perfect, go, sell your possessions, and give the money to the poor, . . . then come, follow me" (Matthew 19:21). The second opening was at the words of Jesus to the apostles when he sent them out to preach: "Take nothing for your journey, no staff, nor bag, nor bread, nor money" (Luke 9:3). The priest opened the missal for the third time and read, "If any want to become my followers, let them deny themselves and take up their cross and follow me" (Mark 8:34). Francis heard these passages as clear advice to Bernard that he should indeed join him in this new life. "Blessed be Jesus Christ," he said, "who has shown us the way to live in accordance with his gospel."

This story shows that Francis did not set out to create something new. He had no intention of creating a particularly "Franciscan" spirituality. He would be at best bemused and at worst horrified to discover that anyone wanted to explore or follow "Franciscan spirituality."

For Francis, and then for Clare, the driving force behind everything they did and said and wrote was a desire to live the gospel—simply that. When Francis wrote the earliest version we have of the Rule, setting out how the men who came to join his brotherhood should live, he started it with the words,

"This is the life of the Gospel of Jesus Christ."[4] In the later, more formal version that was approved by the church, this core remains the same: "The Rule and life of the Friars Minor is this: to observe the holy Gospel of our Lord Jesus Christ by living in obedience, without anything of their own, and in chastity."[5] When Clare came to write her own Rule for her sisters, this is one of the parts of Francis' Rule which that she copied exactly.

In the very simple words, "This is the life of the gospel of Jesus Christ," there are three elements that are central to the Franciscan way.

First, it is a way of life, not simply a way of prayer or of living together or of preaching the gospel, important though all these are. So the Rules of both Francis and Clare are largely concerned with the practicalities of living and working. They wrote about how newcomers joined their community, how those in charge were to act, what kind of work the brothers and sisters might undertake, and how to deal with money, care for the sick, and relate to nonbelievers. Although much of the detail is specific to their time and circumstances, their concern that the whole of life should be lived according to the pattern of the gospel is not.

But it is not just in the Rules that this concern for living can be seen. In his Testament Francis describes those who joined him as "those who came to receive life."[6] And it is not accidental that he goes on immediately to describe how these men "gave to the poor everything they were capable of possessing." The beginning of receiving life was to act, to obey the words of Jesus in the gospel. Just knowing them was not enough.

Francis has stern words for those who seek knowledge alone: "Those . . . are killed by the letter who do not wish to follow the spirit of Sacred Scripture, but only wish to know what the words are and how to interpret them to others."[7]

There are clear parallels here with the epistle of James (1:22-25):

> But be doers of the word, and not merely hearers who deceive themselves. For if any are hearers of the word and not doers, they are like those who look at themselves in a mirror; for they look at themselves and, on going away, immediately forget what they were like. But those who look into the perfect law, the law of liberty, and persevere, being not hearers who forget but doers who act—they will be blessed in their doing.

Francis often quoted from Jesus' words in John's gospel: "The words that I have spoken to you are spirit and life" (6:63). A contemporary of Francis, Odo of Cheriton, heard him say that "he [Francis] was that woman whom the Lord impregnated by his word and thus he brought forth spiritual children."[8] Both John and Peter would recognize this powerful image of the life-giving seed of God, the word, which makes people into God's children (compare 1 John 3:9 and 1 Peter 1:22-23). But the life that Francis believed his hearers would enter through receiving the words of Christ, words that he described as "fragrant," was not simply a gift for the individual, but was to lead to "holy activity."[9]

Launching out into action first, and only later, in the light of experience and reflection, seeking to formalize a program in writing, was a principle of Francis' life. Even the Earlier Rule came together in its final form out of twelve years' experience of seeking to live the life of the gospel. Compared to our current need for detailed business analyses and fully budgeted proposals, Francis' was a radically different way of living.

Richard Rohr, an American Franciscan friar, sums up the two ways very acutely:

> In the final analysis we live our way into a new kind of thinking, but we in the West have always thought we could think our way into a new way of life. You have to run with your own feet to some place where you haven't been before—to a new place.[10]

Francis' feet certainly took him to new places, and in the running he drew many others into new life.

Second, this way of life was the way of life of the gospel. Francis and Clare looked to the group of disciples around Jesus for inspiration. Many other reform movements in the church, then and since, looked back to the very early days of the church recorded in the Acts of the Apostles, and especially to the first chapters of that book. They found their model in Acts 2, in the church in which "all who believed were together and had all things in common. . . . They devoted themselves to the apostles' teaching and fellowship, to the breaking of bread and the prayers" (2:44, 42). But Francis and Clare went back beyond this to the apostles themselves, to those who were around Christ

27

in his three years of active ministry, and to the itinerant, quite unstructured life that they lived.

Francis himself, in his Testament written as he neared death, speaks of this inspiration: "And after the Lord gave me brothers, no one showed me what I should do, but the Most High Himself revealed to me that I should live according to the form of the Holy Gospel."[11] The Rule and the other writings that emerged from this conviction contain many quotations from the Bible, the majority from the gospels, which Francis saw as the blueprint for his way of life.

Even in his method of forming and training his community, Francis followed the way of the gospel. As Jesus called people to follow him, and they learned their new life by being in his company, seeing what he did, and then being sent out to do it themselves, so it was with Francis. His early brothers accompanied him as he traveled, listening to him preach, watching him heal, joining him in service. They must have seemed, to those who met them as they traveled, very like Jesus and his disciples. The friar who compiled the collection of stories known as the Little Flowers, or Fioretti, about a hundred years after Francis' death, makes the comparison explicit in his introduction.

He speaks of Francis beginning with twelve companions, and goes on to draw parallels between certain of the disciples and some of Francis' first followers. Judas has his parallel in John Della Capella, who also apostasized and ended up hanging himself; John the Evangelist has his parallel in Bernard, who, like the Evangelist, attained to divine wisdom. Like the apostles, Francis' first followers possessed nothing but poverty, and their holiness was of a kind not seen since the time of the apostles. Later, Francis began to send his followers out, as Jesus did, and he sent them in pairs, in order to follow perfectly the gospel pattern.

The life of the early Franciscans was very different from the traditional religious life of their day. Members of existing religious communities lived together in monasteries, praying together a number of times a day, working within the monastery and having, as a community, a considerable degree of autonomy. Some communities were large landowners, rich and powerful.

From Chapter 7 of the Earlier Rule, considered to be one of the oldest sections, it seems that the early Franciscans did not live together in houses set aside for them. Instead, they lived among ordinary people, sometimes as part of a household for a time, sometimes on the road, finding shelter where they could at the end of each day. They were not to hold positions of authority or power, but were to take whatever humble work they could. They came together only occasionally to meet each other, share what they had been doing, and be inspired again by Francis. He was very much against the community's acquiring buildings and lands, seeing this as contrary to the spirit of the gospel. After all, had not Jesus spoken of himself as one who had "nowhere to lay his head" (Matthew 8:20)?

The gospel gave Francis his model of mission; it gave him also a powerful and radical model of leadership. As Jesus on the night before he died "got up from the table, took off his outer robe, and tied a towel around himself, . . . poured water into a basin and began to wash the disciples' feet . . ." (John 13:4-5), so Francis washed the feet of the lepers he served. This gospel passage was the one that Francis asked to have read to him as he lay dying. Clare in her turn washed the feet of the sisters who had gone out of the monastery to beg for alms. Both took to heart Jesus' words to his disciples, "You know that the rulers of the Gentiles lord it over them, and their great ones are tyrants over them. It will not be so among you; but whoever wishes to be great among you must be your servant, and whoever wishes to be first among you must be your slave. . . ." (Matthew 20:25-27).

Clare became abbess at San Damiano only very reluctantly. Drawing on the testimony of Sister Pacifica, who knew Clare before she went to San Damiano and joined her there early in the life of the community, the writer of the official life of the new saint says,

> Three years after her conversion, declining the name and office of Abbess, she wished in her humility to be placed under others rather than above them, and, among the servants of Christ, to serve more willingly than to be served. Compelled by blessed Francis, however, she accepted the government of the Ladies, out of which fear, not arrogance, was brought forth from her heart, and freedom did not increase as did service.[12]

Francis, despite being the founder and inspiration of his community, could write, "And I firmly wish to obey the Minister General of this fraternity and another guardian whom it might please him to give me. And I wish to be so captive in his hands that I cannot go anywhere or do anything beyond obedience and his will, for he is my master."[13]

Third, this way of life of the gospel was that of the gospel of Jesus Christ, so both Francis and Clare were intensely Christ-centered. They were seeking to recapture the intimacy of the first disciples with Christ. According to Celano, Francis did achieve this: "He was always occupied with Jesus; Jesus he bore in his heart, Jesus in his mouth, Jesus in his ears, Jesus in his eyes, Jesus in his hands."[14] Bonaventure, who joined the Franciscans in 1243 and became minister general (the leader of the entire Franciscan order), also bore witness to this intense love of Jesus: "When [Francis] pronounced the word 'Jesus' or heard someone say it, he was filled with joy, and he seemed to be completely transformed, as if he had suddenly tasted something marvelous or caught the strain of a beautiful harmony."[15]

For Clare too, following Christ was her central motivation. She spent many years of her life in a struggle with the church authorities over poverty, which she saw as essential to following Christ in a way that remained faithful to Francis' inspiration. In the course of this struggle, one of the popes offered to absolve her, to free her, from the very strict poverty that she had taken on. Clare replied, "Absolve me from my sins, but not from following Christ." The document that Pope Innocent III gave to Clare allowing her to take on such poverty speaks of Clare and her sisters as clinging in all things to Christ's footprints.

Her writings are intoxicated with the love of Christ. In her letters to Agnes of Prague, a Bohemian princess who, inspired by the friars who reached Prague in 1225, founded a house of the Poor Ladies there, Clare wrote often of Christ as the spouse of those who choose to live for him,

> Whose power is stronger,
> Whose generosity is more abundant,
> Whose appearance more beautiful,
> Whose love more tender,
> Whose courtesy more gracious.
> In Whose embrace you are already caught up.[16]

In fact, one summary of Franciscan spirituality goes like this: "Christ in the crib, Christ on the cross, Christ in the Eucharist." Always Christ, and Christ present to us.

It was his desire to bring home to people that nearness of Christ that led Francis to create the first Christmas crib. At a small town called Greccio, in December 1223, he asked a man named John to prepare a manger, with hay, an ox, and an ass. Then Francis, his brothers, and the local people came at Christmas with great rejoicing to celebrate the birth, and Francis preached "concerning the nativity of the poor King."[17] His words were undoubtedly powerful, but Francis sought always to incarnate, to flesh out, his message in ways that made them more powerful still.

Clare too had a warm devotion to the Christ-child. Several of her sisters testified that they had seen the child Jesus come close to Clare in a vision. This devotion spilt over into her ministry. Over half of the healings ascribed to her in her lifetime were of children, and this continued after her death. Tender devotion to the child became a hallmark of Franciscan spirituality.

The Fioretti tells the story of Brother Conrad praying to Mary that he might feel a little of the sweetness that Simeon had felt when he held Christ in his arms in the temple. Then, we are told, Mary appeared, carrying Christ in her arms. She placed her son in the arms of Brother Conrad, "who received him with tenderest devotion, embracing and kissing him and pressing him to his breast."[18]

The humanity of Christ is at the heart of Franciscan spirituality, but it is not expressed only in what might seem a sentimental attachment to the baby in the manger. Francis and Clare never forgot that the incarnation was costly, but they saw the cost in rather different ways. Francis focused on the self-emptying of Christ in obedience to the Father, and so wrote much of obedience and humility. For him a key passage was from Philippians (2:5-8):

> Let the same mind be in you that was in Christ Jesus,
>> who, though he was in the form of God,
>>> did not regard equality with God
>>> as something to be exploited,
>> but emptied himself,
>>> taking the form of a slave,
>>> being born in human likeness.
>> And being found in human form,
>>> he humbled himself
>>> and became obedient to the point of death—
>>> even death on a cross.

Clare, on the other hand, focused on the generosity and poverty of Christ: "For you know the generous act of our Lord Jesus Christ, that though he was rich, yet for your sakes he became poor, so that by his poverty you might become rich" (2 Corinthians 8:9); therefore she stressed the preeminent role of poverty for her sisters.

As Paul wrote to the Philippians, the cost of the incarnation extended beyond Bethlehem to Calvary, and a deep devotion to the passion of Christ was also central for both Francis and Clare—literally central in one of Clare's most striking images, that of the mirror. In her teaching on prayer, she encouraged her sisters to gaze on Christ as on a mirror. At the very heart of the mirror she placed the passion of Christ: "In the depths of this . . . mirror, contemplate the ineffable charity which led Him to suffer on the wood of the Cross and die thereon the most shameful kind of death."[19]

"Christ in the crib, Christ on the cross, Christ in the Eucharist." In the Eucharist the Christ who came as a baby and died on the cross is still with us. Francis marveled at this and called all to do the same. In a letter to all his followers, he wrote,

> O admirable heights and sublime lowliness!
> O sublime humility!
> O humble sublimity!
> That the Lord of the universe,
> God and the Son of God,
>   so humbles himself
>   that for our salvation
> He hides Himself under the little form of bread![20]

And so he exhorted all his brothers "to show all possible reverence and honor to the most holy Body and Blood of our Lord Jesus Christ."[21] He wanted this reverence to be worked out even in the small details of worship. In a letter to the clergy, he asked them to keep clean the chalices and altar cloths that were used in the Eucharist.

But he did not separate word and sacrament; at the same time as pleading with his brothers, clergy, and the whole church to treat with reverence the sacrament of Christ's body and blood, he asked them to treat with equal reverence and care the word of God, which consecrated and made holy the bread and wine, which made present again Christ, the Word of God: "Wherever the written words of the Lord may be found in unbecoming places, they are to be collected and kept in a place that is becoming."[22]

Clare, too, placed a high value on God's word, both in Scripture and in sermons. When, in a papal Bull (a solemn edict) of 1230, Pope Gregory forbade the brothers to go to the Poor Clare monasteries as they had been accustomed to doing, Clare was distressed at the loss of preaching that this would mean. In a powerful and effective protest, she sent away the brothers who had been begging food on behalf of the sisters, saying, "Let him now take away from us all the brothers, since he has taken away those who provide us with the food that is vital."[23] When the pope heard this, he allowed the minister general of the brothers freedom to interpret the Bull, and the preaching brothers were restored to the sisters.

The word that spoke of Christ, the Word; the incarnation and passion in which they saw his humility, generosity, and love; the sacrament of bread and wine in which they received him, were at the very heart of the spiritual lives of Francis and Clare. And so it is not surprising that there are so many quotations from the Bible, nearly four hundred in all, half of them from the gospels, in the Rules, Testaments, and other writings of both Francis and Clare. But how would they have come to know the Bible? And are there any lessons we can learn today from how they chose to use it?

Francis and Clare lived before the invention of printing and before the widespread translation of the Bible into languages other than Latin. So the Bible as a book was not widely available to most people. One copy cost about as much as a horse, and the words of the Bible were not directly available to those who didn't read Latin, which was the language of the clergy. Francis remained a layman all his life, and all the evidence points to his Latin being weak. Bonaventure, who joined the Franciscans less than twenty years after Francis' death, writes of his education that he "had got a slight knowledge of reading and writing."[24] Francis himself often refers to his use of someone else to write down his letters and prayers. From his biographies we know of four secretaries.

Most people therefore did not own a Bible, and would not have been able to read it if they had. Bibles were found largely in churches, and it was one of the tasks of the priest to translate the readings into the local language, and to explain them to his hearers. Several of the stories from the early days of Francis and his community reflect this.

When, on St. Matthias' Day 1208, Francis went to Mass and heard Christ's words sending his disciples out to preach, "shortly afterwards, having understood these words more fully, thanks to the priest himself, he was filled with unspeakable joy. This, he said, is exactly what I am looking for, this is what I desire from the bottom of my heart." The fuller understanding probably came through the priest's translation of the words of the gospel into Italian.

And when Bernard went with Francis to church to see if it was God's will for him to join this new brotherhood, they asked the priest to open the book for them, not in a random way, but seeking particular texts. They had heard them before, and knew that they spoke powerfully to them of God's call—but they didn't know where to find them in the Bible.

These two stories make it clear that in the early days the main place in which Francis and his companions heard the words of Scripture was at the Mass, the Eucharist—and that the emphasis was very much on hearing, not on private reading. This remained the case as the order grew. A story tells that the first New Testament the brothers ever owned was given away to a poor woman, so that she could sell it and buy food. This happened in about 1220, when the order was around ten years old and had more than 5,000 members. The rarity and value of the Bible is also reflected in a story of Francis dividing the pages of a New Testament among the brothers so that all could read a portion.

It is not surprising in the light of this, that the actual words of Scripture were very precious to Francis, and early stories tell of him picking up the written word with reverence and placing even scraps of paper in a safe place. As we have seen, in a letter to the clergy Francis asked them to treat the words of the gospels in particular with the same reverence that they give to the bread and wine of the Eucharist.

Francis' emphasis was on a literal living out of the gospel, and he sometimes applied the words of the gospel to the details of everyday life in a very concrete way that seems slightly ridiculous today. The brothers did not put the beans for the next day's meal to soak the night before, as most people did, because Jesus had said, "Do not worry about tomorrow" (Matthew 6:34). More seriously, when they went out begging, they would never accept more money than they needed for that day.

But in fact Francis' way of using the Bible was more subtle than these stories suggest. Perhaps "realist" is a better way of describing it than "literal." He was always concerned with the spirit as much as the letter, and quotes with approval, "The letter kills, but the spirit gives life" (2 Corinthians 3:6, in Admonition 7). Sometimes in his concern for the spirit he went beyond the letter, as in his response to the passage from Matthew's gospel in which Jesus sent out his disciples to preach (the passage he heard on St. Matthias' Day): "As you go, proclaim the good news. . . . You received without payment, give without payment. Take no gold, or silver, or copper in your belts, no bag for your journey, or two tunics, or sandals, or a staff" (Matthew 10:7, 8-10). Christ told his disciples not to take two tunics—but Francis disposed of both of his and made himself a rough garment; Christ told his disciples not to take any coins in their belt—but Francis cast aside his belt altogether and replaced it with a cord, which was what the peasants wore. His was not necessarily a literal response, but a wholehearted one that took seriously both the words and the spirit of the gospel.

Always his interest was in the practical, in action, in living the words. There were other ways open to him. Some of his contemporaries, including his biographers, built complex layers of symbolism around the texts they used, or constructed elaborate allegories in which everything stood for something else. For example, the passage from Matthew to which Francis responded in such a practical way was also interpreted in this way: "The two tunics symbolize duplicity; the sandals, which are made from the skins of dead animals, signify fraudulent execution of wills; and the staff denotes the excessive appetite for power."[25]

In contrast, Francis remained simple and practical before the gospel, and perhaps this is his lesson for those who follow him today. Hearing or reading the Bible was never for him a purely academic or intellectual exercise. It was an encounter with the living God who called him always to conversion and to action. ❧

Chapter 3

God's Holy Manner of Working

Francis and Clare shared so much—a passion for living the gospel, a deep devotion to Christ, an unwavering commitment to poverty, a dedication to the service of others. You might expect that they spent much time together, encouraging each other and sharing plans for the future. But in fact, once Clare had settled at San Damiano they saw very little of each other. Francis was out on the road, traveling, preaching, meeting with his brothers; Clare was building up the community at San Damiano. She was dependent on Francis' visits, and he seems to have been wary of visiting too often.

But on one occasion when he was staying in Assisi for a time, he did visit Clare at San Damiano to talk with her. She wanted very much to eat with him, but for a long time he refused. His brothers urged him to be generous to the woman who had given up so much to follow Christ in his way, and finally he relented. Not only did he agree to have a meal with Clare, but he suggested that they should go together to St. Mary of the Angels, where she had joined Francis on the night she ran away from home, and where she had received the habit.

So on the appointed day, Clare, with one of her sisters, was escorted by some of the brothers to St. Mary of the Angels, where the meal was prepared. As the first course was being

served, Francis began to talk of God, and he did this so beautifully, so sweetly, and with such a sense of the majesty of God,
that they were all caught up in God's grace, and went into a
rapture.

Meanwhile, the local people saw great flames leaping from
the chapel, the house, and even the forest that surrounded
them. Alarmed, they came rushing to St. Mary of the Angels.
But when they arrived they found no fire, but only Francis and
Clare and their companions, their eyes and hands raised to
heaven, aflame in the contemplation of God.

This is a powerful image of all-consuming prayer. Fire is
found a number of times in the Bible as an image of God's
presence. The tongues of fire that came down on the apostles
at Pentecost, and Moses meeting God in the burning bush, are
probably the most familiar examples. Both of these stories are
reflected in a story about Francis. Brother Leo, one of Francis'
closest companions, saw a flame of fire descend and rest on
Francis' head on Mount Alverna, where Francis was spending
a prolonged retreat. Francis told Leo afterwards that the flame
was God, who spoke to him as he did to Moses.

Stories such as these are our main way of learning about how
Francis and Clare prayed. Neither of them wrote any treatises,
though some later Franciscans, such as Bonaventure, did. Neither of them seems to have taught a system. We have to glean
what we can from the stories told about them, from the written
prayers that have survived, and from the provision for prayer
made in their Rules. These different sources, like the many facets of a diamond, show us different aspects of the way Francis
and Clare prayed and the effects their prayer had on their lives.

A deep life of prayer was the jewel at the heart of their lives, a jewel that reflected light onto a number of elements of the spiritual life, some obviously linked closely to prayer, some rather more surprising.

In this, as in so many ways, they are very like Jesus. He too left no handbook of prayer, no formal system of meditation. We have the evidence of the gospels that prayer was an essential part of his life. We have the few prayers recorded in the gospels. But above all, we have the evidence of a life lived in communion with the Father. This was the aim of Francis and Clare, too.

Perhaps such a deep life of prayer will always lead to reticence. Words fail, and only silence seems appropriate. But there are also cultural reasons for their comparative silence about their own prayer. A writer on Clare points out that she and Francis lived in a period where the communal dimension had priority over the individual, and where self-awareness had a much lower priority than it has now. "To ask how an individual prays presupposes not only an interest in the self, but also the vocabulary for describing individual experience. Clare of Assisi had neither."[26]

However, we are fortunate that Clare's life of prayer was lived in the confines of the monastery at San Damiano. The sisters who lived with her there, some for many years, were questioned shortly after Clare's death, when the church was considering declaring her a saint. Their answers were written down and have survived.

These sisters spoke of Clare's fervor in prayer. Sister Amata said, "She was assiduous in prayer and contemplation. When she returned from prayer, her face appeared clearer and more beautiful than the sun."[27] Again we may be reminded of Moses, whose face shone when he had been speaking with God (Exodus 34:29-35; 2 Corinthians 3:7). Sister Benvenuta, who joined the community only a few months after Clare herself, said, "In that place where the Lady Clare usually went to pray, she saw above it a great brilliance so she believed it was the flame of an actual fire."[28] Sister Pacifica, who also joined the community in the very early days, said that Clare was "assiduous and careful in her prayers, lying a long time upon the ground, remaining humbly prostrate."[29]

They also spoke of her compassion and deep feeling. Sister Filippa: "The blessed mother had especially the gift of many tears, having great compassion for the sisters and the afflicted. She especially poured out many tears when she received the Body of our Lord Jesus Christ."[30]

Many of the witnesses spoke of her curing illnesses through prayer and the sign of the cross, among the sisters and among those who came to the monastery. Prayer was Clare's natural response to any need, from a shortage of food for the sisters, to the threat posed by a marauding army. On two occasions the city of Assisi and the monastery were threatened with invasion—once by an army of Saracens, who actually scaled the wall and came into the monastery, and once by the troops of Emperor Frederick II. When the Saracens invaded, Clare comforted her sisters, assuring them that Jesus would free them. Then she turned to prayer, and the Saracens "departed away as if driven away without doing any harm nor touching anyone in the house."[31] When the emperor's troops threatened Assisi, the people called on Clare to help. She in turn called on her sisters, placing ashes on their heads as a sign of penitence. Then they all went to the chapel to pray, and many of them fasted all day. That army, too, left without doing any harm.

For Francis, the evidence is a little less direct, as we would expect when so much of his life was spent on the move. But there are many stories of the hours he spent in prayer; of how easily moved to prayer he was; of the priority that prayer had in his life. Thomas of Celano says that "walking, sitting, eating, or drinking, he was always intent upon prayer."[32] He tells how Francis would divide his time between the service of others and the contemplation of God, often seeking out deserted churches and lonely places for his prayer. He prayed particularly when there was a decision to be made, spending many hours coming into God's presence and seeking his will. He had a particular devotion to the cross and would be drawn into prayer not only by the crosses and crucifixes in churches or set up by the roadside, but even by the crossed branches of a tree. Like Clare, he experienced both great joy and great sorrow in prayer, dancing and singing, but also weeping for his sins and the sins of the world.

When it comes to written prayers, however, the balance of the evidence changes. We have very few, if any, actual prayers of Clare's, but a number from Francis. Assuming that what they wrote reflects their own life of prayer, what can we learn from Francis' prayers about how he prayed?

One of the earliest prayers, and the shortest, contains many of the elements found in the later and longer ones. It also holds a special place as the prayer Francis recommended to his brothers when they asked him, "How shall we pray?" Along with the Our Father, he told them to say this prayer. In particular, they were to say it whenever they entered a church or saw one from a distance, and whenever they saw a cross or anything in the shape of a cross:

> We adore you, most holy Lord Jesus Christ,
> here, and in all your churches throughout all the world;
> and we bless you
> because, by your holy cross,
> you have redeemed the world.[33]

The prayer begins with adoration, adoration of Christ; it names churches as particular places where God may be met; and it centers on the cross as the means of redemption. These were all central themes in Francis' life. For prayer, the first is the most crucial.

Adoration and praise were at the heart of prayer for Francis. The focus was always on God, on God as Most High, holy, good—these words recur many times in his prayers. Almost the only petitions Francis made were to know God's will and to be able to carry it out. But even these prayers began in praise. They were personal, addressing God directly, often using the familiar form of "you" in the original Latin or Italian. They became increasingly simple as his life went on, reflecting, we may imagine, a way of prayer in which words became increasingly unnecessary.

Two years before his death, Francis wrote this prayer of thanksgiving and gave it to Brother Leo:

You are holy, Lord, the only God,
    and your deeds are wonderful.
You are strong, you are great.
You are the Most High, you are almighty.
You, holy Father, are King of heaven and earth.
You are Three and One, Lord God, all good.
You are Good, all Good, supreme Good,
    Lord God, living and true.
You are love, you are wisdom.
You are humility, you are endurance.
You are rest, you are peace.
You are joy and gladness.
You are justice and moderation.
You are all our riches and you suffice for us.
You are beauty, you are gentleness.
You are our protector,
    you are our guardian and defender.
You are courage, you are our haven and our hope.
You are our faith, our great consolation.
You are our eternal life, great and wonderful Lord,
    God almighty, merciful Savior.[34]

With its repetition of "you, you, you" this is the prayer of a
man totally focused on God, finding in God all he could want.
Beginning with pure praise of God for who he is—holy, Most
High, Father, King, all good—it moves on to God's qualities—
love, wisdom, humility, joy, justice, beauty—and finally on
to who he is for us—our protector, guardian, defender, courage, haven, hope, consolation: in fact, all our riches. It is even

more striking when we realize that it was written at a time when Francis was ill, in pain from the stigmata, the wounds of the crucifixion, which he had received in his own body during a time of deep prayer. He was still presumably struggling to come to terms with what had happened to him. It is a marvelous testimony to his ability to transcend all that might have distracted him from prayer, and simply to worship.

This call to worship, to universal worship, became increasingly the focus of Francis' prayer over the years. But the very first prayer, in fact his very first recorded words, are much more personal. They are the words he said before the crucifix in the abandoned church of San Damiano, while he was serving the lepers:

> Most High, glorious God,
> enlighten the darkness of my heart
> and give me, Lord,
> a correct faith,
> a certain hope,
> a perfect charity,
> sense and knowledge,
> so that I may carry out Your holy and true command.[35]

Francis was twenty-three when he used this prayer, and it is very much one of personal relationship with God—my heart, give me, so that I may carry out. Later in his life, when the way had become clearer, his prayer changed and became a call to all of creation to praise its Creator, to join in the worship of heaven. In the "Praises Before the Office," for example, we find,

> Praise him in his glory, heaven and earth,
> and every creature that is in heaven and on the earth
> and under the earth and such as are on the seas,
> and all that are in them.[36]

Nothing is left out of the universal call to praise God. This prayer, like many others, uses many images and phrases, words and quotations from the Bible. Francis prays God's word back to God.

And it is Jesus' own words that stand at the center of what has been called Francis' "catechism of prayer." He wrote a prayer based on the Our Father, a common enough practice at his time. His, however, is distinctive enough to be likely to reflect something of his own prayer. There is a strong sense that God's gifts are at the heart of all we can do for him:

> You give them [the angels and the saints] light so that they may have knowledge, because you are light. You inflame them so that they may love, because you are love. You live continually in them so that they may be happy.[37]

We are called to a totality of giving,

> That we may love you with our whole heart by always thinking of you; with our whole mind by directing our whole intention towards you and seeking your glory in everything; and with all our strength by spending all our energies and affec-

tions of soul and body in the service of your love
alone.[38]

But the reward of such self-giving is equally total; we will
be brought to God's kingdom, "where we shall see you clearly,
love you perfectly, be happy in your company and enjoy you
for ever."[39]

Clare has left only one written prayer—a blessing for her sisters, present and to come. But in her letters to Agnes of Prague,
we have some evidence of the content of that passionate prayer
to which her sisters witnessed. It is characterized by warmth
and light, expressive of a deeply felt devotion to Christ. Francis
called upon all the world to praise God and to give him honor
and glory. Appropriately for one committed to the interior life
of enclosure and prayer, Clare called on her sisters to give all of
themselves. The call to totality is the same, but where Francis
extended it outward to the entire created order, Clare directed
it inward to the depths of each human person.

Clare's life of contemplation is characterized by the word
"gaze"—*considerare* in the original Latin. It is at the heart of
her spirituality, as seen in the letters to Agnes, and so we may
suppose it was at the heart of her own prayer life. Those long
hours in prayer, from which she returned with her face clear
and bright, must have contained much simple gazing on God in
the person of Christ. This adoring gaze flowed over into all the
activities of her day.

In her Rule, echoing some words of Francis, she exhorts the
sisters to work in such a way that "they do not extinguish the
Spirit of holy prayer and devotion to which all other things of

our earthly existence must contribute."[40] Desire for God was at the heart of her life and was what she counseled for others. Writing to Ermentrude of Bruges, the founder of several monasteries in Flanders, she gave the simple instruction, "Love God from the depths of your heart and Jesus, His Son, Who was crucified for us sinners. Never let the thought of Him leave your mind."[41]

Mind, soul and heart were all to be involved:

> Place your mind before the mirror of eternity!
> Place your soul in the brilliance of glory!
> Place your heart in the image of the divine substance![42]

Her readers were to gather up all that was in them and bring it before God, deliberately placing themselves in God's presence. The results of such activity were marvelous:

> By such contemplation we are renewed,
> by such kindliness flooded,
> by such sweetness filled,
> We are gently enlightened by such a memory.[43]

This prayer was not passive—it was deliberate, intentional, chosen. It was to become a habitual practice and attitude of mind, permeating all of life and affecting everything else. Frances Teresa OSC speaks of a "whole program of prayer summarized in a series of verbs" in Clare's last letter to Agnes, written shortly before her death:

Look into this mirror of Christ daily,
ponder there your own face,
see what you need to become ready for God,
contemplate in this mirror Christ and
        his stupendous poverty,
look at his work on our behalf,
consider his humility,
contemplate his love,
consider, look, and contemplate.[44]

The image of the mirror is one that Clare used often—on what do we gaze in our prayer? On Christ, who reflects God. What is the effect of this prayer? We come in our turn to reflect Christ to the world. The mirror was a common image in medieval spirituality, but Clare uses it in a particularly rich way.

As with so much in Franciscan writing on prayer, what Clare wrote is not systematic, and can at times seem quite confusing. But the controlling idea is that of Christ at the center of prayer. Clare then unfolds a variety of ways of relating to that center as she develops the image in her letters to Agnes.

In the second letter the call is to gaze, consider, contemplate—in proportion as Agnes desires to imitate God. The mirror image has not yet appeared, but the idea of gazing on God in order to be transformed into God's likeness is there.

In the third letter comes this passage, already quoted:

Place your mind before the mirror of eternity!
Place your soul in the brilliance of glory!
Place your heart in the image of the divine substance![45]

And then Clare goes on, "And transform your whole being into the image of the Godhead Itself, through contemplation!"[46]

Prayer is powerful, affecting mind, soul, and heart. Prayer is powerful, effecting transformation. Prayer is powerful, able to restore us to the image of God in which we were created (Genesis 1:26).

In the fourth letter comes the most extended use of the mirror metaphor. The vision of Christ is described in glowing language, ending with two phrases taken from Scripture. This vision is the "splendor of eternal glory" (Hebrews 1:3) and "the brilliance of eternal light and the mirror without blemish" (Wisdom 7:26).[47] Then Agnes is exhorted to look into that mirror every day, to see first herself. This will enable her to do what is needed to cover herself "with the flowers and garments of all the virtues"[48]—virtues that can themselves be seen in the mirror.

Then the image becomes more complex, and it is necessary to know a little about medieval mirrors to make sense of Clare's next section. She counsels Agnes to look at the mirror itself, and in its three different parts to see reflected aspects of Christ's life. We are not accustomed to looking at mirrors for themselves, and we expect to see the same image reflected in all parts of the mirror. But medieval mirrors were not made of glass, but of bronze; and they were not flat, but slightly convex on one side. Thus they reflected in different ways at different points on the mirror, and only certain parts of the mirror reflected the image clearly.

So Clare sees, at the borders of the mirror, the poverty and humility of the incarnation. At the surface, she sees Christ's life on earth, also marked by humility and by poverty. In the depths, where the reflection is clearest, she sees the passion, motivated by love. Then, in another change of image, she sees Christ himself as the mirror "suspended on the wood of the Cross"[49] and calling on those who pass by to "look and see if there is any suffering like My suffering!" (Lamentations 1:12). A variety of images, but always the call to look, to contemplate.

There is also the call to be mirrors, reflecting God. In the Testament she wrote near the end of her life, Clare speaks of herself and her sisters at the center of a series of reflections. At the beginning is God, and particularly God as seen in Christ, who is the Way. Francis saw this first, and then reflected it to Clare. She in her turn reflected Christ to her sisters and to the world outside. She and her present sisters together are to be mirrors to those who come to join the community, "so that they in turn will be a mirror and example to those living in the world."[50] This "mirroring" is a strong incentive for their life: "Since, therefore, the Lord has called us to such great things, that those who are to be models and mirrors for others may behold themselves in us, we are truly bound to bless and praise the Lord and to be strengthened constantly in Him to do good."[51]

Clare uses the same language in speaking of both poverty and love, which were at the heart of her life. Clare learned poverty from God, through Francis, and has formed those who live with her in it, so that they too may teach it to others. They are to have Christ's love in their hearts and show it outwardly in their deeds, so that others may grow in this love and in their turn show it to others.

The image of the mirror speaks of a kind of infectious spirituality, in which what is seen in prayer, in gazing, in contemplation, effects a transformation in the life of the one who gazes, so that others may be drawn by what they see in her to their own contemplation and to their own transformation.

So far, we have been looking at private prayer. But the context of all of Clare's prayer, as of Francis', was the common prayer of the church, the Divine Office, continuing day in and day out. This is the next facet of the jewel. For Clare and her sisters, the prayer in common took place in their chapel at San Damiano; for Francis and his brothers, it took place wherever they could find somewhere to stop for a time on the road. But both made provision in their Rules for this prayer, adapting it as necessary to the capacity of those praying. Those who could read were to use the books provided by the church; those who could not were to say prayers that they knew by heart, principally the Creed and the Our Father. Clare specified that the office was to be said, not sung, in contrast to most other communities of women. In fact, this public prayer in common is the only prayer legislated for in the Rules, presumably because it was important in this area to conform to the custom of the church.

For private prayer, Francis and Clare were themselves the example and rule to their brothers and sisters. Their own lives of prayer were sufficient instruction. A story of the early days of Francis and his brothers shows that private prayer was an essential and accepted part of their lives. For a time they lived near Assisi at a place called Rivo Torto. Their home was an abandoned hovel, and they lived very simply, often lacking bread and living on turnips, for which they begged. In addition, the hovel was very cramped. But Francis wrote the names of the brothers on the beams so that each would know where he might find a small space to pray or rest.

We can imagine that many of their prayers were seeking God's will for them. Were they really meant to be living so hard a life? Would it not be better to be running churches, preaching the word as respected priests, not despised friars, apparently not making a difference? In these circumstances it is easy to see why, for the early Franciscans, seeking God's will—discernment—was the mainspring of their prayer. Discernment, and the role of the Holy Spirit in the spiritual life, is the next facet of the jewel.

Francis and Clare believed that God's will would as often be revealed through the prayers of others as by their own prayer. In the early days, Francis was struggling to decide whether he should devote his life to prayer, or whether he should also preach. He must have prayed often about this dilemma, but he also asked Clare and one of his brothers, Silvester, to pray for him. He sent Brother Masseo to these two to ask their prayers and to bring back the answer.

On Masseo's return, Francis received him with honor as God's messenger, washing his feet and preparing a meal for him. Then he knelt down, stretched out his arms in the form of a cross, and asked, "What does my Lord Jesus Christ command that I should do?" Then Masseo told him that both Clare and Silvester had said that he should go out into the world and preach. Francis received this as God's word for him, and immediately set out to fulfill God's will.

This was, after all, where he had started, with the simple prayer, "Lord, what do you want me to do?" And his first recorded prayer, before the crucifix at San Damiano, as we have seen, asks for enlightenment of the heart, for faith, hope, and love, so that Francis may carry out God's will. Clare picks up a phrase from this prayer when speaking of her own conversion in her Testament, giving thanks that God "enlightened her heart" to do penance and to follow Francis in leaving everything and embarking on a life of poverty. It turned out to be crucial that she had her own sense of God's leading, because although from the beginning she committed herself entirely to Francis' guidance, she lived many years after his death, and had to find her own way of following in the unfolding circumstances and difficulties of life at San Damiano. Perhaps this was part of Francis' wisdom in leaving her often alone at San Damiano, and not visiting as often as she would have wished. She was forced back into that intimate and delicate process of waiting on God, learning to interpret the stirrings of the soul as messages from him.

For Clare in particular, visions and prophecy were an important source for knowing God's will. In part this was due to the conditions of the time. Women could not preach or carry out any of the duties of priests, and they were forbidden to lead an itinerant life. But visions and prophecy were believed to come directly from the Holy Spirit, and could not therefore be forbidden. Prophecies had informed Clare's life from before her birth. Her sisters knew of the words heard by her mother while pregnant with her. Clare herself put great weight on the prophecy made by Francis while rebuilding San Damiano and included it in detail in her Testament. She specifically says that these were the words of God, spoken through Francis. And Clare herself saw a number of visions, which she told to some of her sisters.

For the brothers too, visions and prophecies were an accepted part of the spiritual life. We have seen their role in Francis' early life in Chapter 1. But there are many other stories.

Brother Silvester, whose advice Francis sought, had seen a vision before he joined the brothers. He saw Francis with a cross of gold coming out of his mouth, a cross so large that the top touched heaven and the arms reached to the ends of the world. While Francis was at prayer with some of the brothers, as they spoke in turn, Christ appeared to them and blessed them. Francis himself knew what the brothers did even when he was absent from them, and he was often given a supernatural knowledge of the secrets of their hearts. At his death, one of his brothers saw his soul ascending to heaven, like a star, taken upward on a white cloud. Another saw him, dressed as a deacon, entering heaven and feasting with his brothers already there. And it seemed to the crowd gathered to welcome Francis, and to the brother who had the vision, that Christ and Francis were one and the same person. Francis was so focused on Christ that he had realized to an extraordinary degree Paul's words to the Galatians, "It is no longer I who live, but it is Christ who lives in me" (2:20). Francis had disappeared, and only Christ was left. Brother James of La Massa, some time after Francis' death, had a vision of the Franciscan order as a tree. Each branch represented a province, and the fruits on each branch were the friars of that province. Christ called Francis to him, and gave him a chalice, full of the Spirit of life, sending him to offer it to his brothers.

Such communication from God may seem strange to us, but

it is very scriptural. The prophets in particular gained many of their insights into God and his workings from visions. "What do you see, Amos?" is a regular refrain in the book of that prophet. Amos recounts what he sees, and God interprets it to him. Paul was famously converted by a vision of Christ on the road to Damascus (Acts 9). The next chapter of Acts is also shaped by visions: first Cornelius' vision of Christ, who tells him to send for Peter; then Peter's vision of the sheet let down from heaven, and the words he hears declaring all the animals in it clean. So he is persuaded that the Gentiles are called by God in the same way as the Jews. Prompted by the Spirit, he goes with Cornelius' messengers, and Cornelius and all his family are filled with the Holy Spirit through Peter's preaching. In the book of Revelation, John, in the Spirit, sees and hears what he is to write in his book. Francis, Clare, and the early Franciscans were in a well-authenticated tradition.

Biblically, prophecy and vision are seen as one of the gifts of the Spirit. "I will pour out my spirit on all flesh; your sons and your daughters shall prophesy, your old men shall dream dreams, and your young men shall see visions" (Joel 2:28). Peter sees these words as being fulfilled on the day of Pentecost (Acts 2:17).

Bonaventure speaks of Clare as "schooled by the Holy Spirit," and the same could undoubtedly have been said of Francis. Thomas of Celano tells us that Francis considered the Holy Spirit the minister general of the order. Both Francis and Clare speak of their own call and the call of their brothers and sisters as being by "divine inspiration," emphasizing the central role of the Holy Spirit in the very beginnings of the Franciscan life. Both write of God's "holy manner of working," a phrase always linked closely to the work of the Spirit. Francis, for example, in a letter written to all the faithful, speaks of them (picking up Jesus' own words) as children of the Father, and spouses, brothers, and mothers of Christ. How do we become spouses of Christ? When our souls are joined to Jesus, our Lord, by the Holy Spirit. How do we become mothers of Christ? When we give birth to him through his "holy manner of working," as we carry him in both our hearts and bodies through love and a pure conscience.[52] In our openness to the work of the Spirit within us, we become, like Mary, God-bearers to the world.

It is noticeable that both speak of the Spirit of the Lord—it is Christ's Spirit that enables them to follow him, not just externally following in the style of his life, though that is demanding enough, but being animated from within by the Holy Spirit, the Spirit of Christ, dwelling within. This is, of course, a very Pauline concept. "God has sent the Spirit of his Son into our hearts" (Galatians 4:6); "But you are not in the flesh; you are in the Spirit, since the Spirit of God dwells in you. Anyone who does not have the Spirit of Christ does not belong to him" (Romans 8:9).

There are two facets of this indwelling of the Spirit, both very important. On the one hand, it is only the presence of the Spirit that enables us to see and believe in the Christ, the Word made flesh: "The Holy Spirit, whom the Father will send in my name, will teach you everything, and remind you of all that I have said to you" (John 14:26). On the other, it is the Spirit within who shapes us into the form of Christ, in whose image we have been created. In our bodies we image Christ; through the Spirit of the Lord we are to be animated to live his life. It is a startling concept, a high calling, but for Francis this is God's work within us, and not something in which we are to take pride. Instead it is another cause for gratitude.

Francis also reflects Paul's writing on the life of the Spirit and the life of the flesh. In both of his Rules there are sections contrasting these two ways of life in terms very reminiscent of Galatians 5:16-24. Life in the flesh is self-centered; life in the Spirit is centered on others and on God.

But paradoxically, the other-centered life of the Spirit is also the way of freedom. Paul writes, "Where the Spirit of the Lord is, there is freedom" (2 Corinthians 3:17). The call of Francis and Clare was not to exact conformity with a set of rules and regulations, but to walk in a way. This was shown in small ways. For example, both made provision in their Rules for the habit that the brothers or sisters were to wear. But both also allowed those in authority to change this provision. Clare wrote, "The Abbess shall provide them with clothing prudently, according to the needs of each person and place, and seasons and cold climates."[53] Similarly with food, there were regulations about fasting, but also, "And they may eat whatever food is placed before them."[54] As so often, Francis supported this with a quotation from the gospels, here Luke 10:8.

But it was not just in the practical details of life that this freedom applied. Two texts from Francis speak powerfully of the freedom of each Christian to follow in Christ's footsteps in his or her own way. One is in a short letter to Brother Leo, one of his closest companions. Francis counseled him, "In whatever way it seems best to you to please the Lord God and to follow His footprints and His poverty, do this with the blessing of God and my obedience."[55] The touchstone was not following Francis and his Rule, but pleasing God and following in Christ's footprints, in poverty.

The second text is recorded by Thomas of Celano. Francis, dying, said to the brothers gathered around him, "I have done what was mine to do; may Christ teach you what you are to do."[56] Again he pointed away from himself, and toward Christ. There are many ways to walk after Christ the Teacher. What matters is to find one's own way and to walk in it faithfully. The Spirit is essential to this exploration, and to the life that springs from it.

Therefore, it is not surprising that both Francis and Clare stressed in their Rules the need to have the Spirit of the Lord above all else. Interestingly, both did so in the context of those who could not read. The brothers and sisters who were illiterate were not to fret about this, or be eager to learn, thinking that this would improve their spiritual life. Instead they were to pursue "what they must desire above all things: to have the Spirit of the Lord and His holy manner of working."[57] Perhaps there is a lesson here for all of us who think, "I would pray much better if only I could . . . ." Prayer, for Francis and Clare, was a gift of the Spirit, and their only desire was to have that Spirit. Everything else would come from that.

Again, this is very biblical. Many of the New Testament writers see prayer as animated by the Spirit, and for Francis as well as for them, prayer is one of the primary manifestations of the Spirit's presence within us: "The hour is coming, and is now here, when the true worshippers will worship the Father in spirit and truth" (John 4:23); "We do not know how to pray as we ought, but that very Spirit intercedes with sighs too deep for words" (Romans 8:26); "Be filled with the Spirit, as you sing psalms and hymns and spiritual songs among yourselves" (Ephesians 5:18-19).

Celano has a striking image when he writes of Francis "not so much praying as becoming himself a prayer."[58] Perhaps this is something of what Paul was envisioning when he wrote about praying "without ceasing" (1 Thessalonians 5:17). Certainly prayer for Francis was not meant to be an escape from the realities of life, a way of floating away into an other-worldly sphere. We can see this in Chapter V of his Later Rule, about work, which the brothers are to do in such a way that "they do not extinguish the Spirit of holy prayer and devotion to which all other things of our earthly existence must contribute."[59] We have already seen that Clare copied these words exactly into her Rule. The realities of life were to contribute to prayer, to be taken into it, not to be left behind or denied by it. Christ was to be discovered as much in the mundane realities of work and life with others as in the beauties of creation or the pleasures of solitude.

For both Francis and Clare, Mary, the mother of Christ, was a model of life lived in the Spirit. Francis addressed her as "the Spouse of the Holy Spirit,"[60] the one who surrendered herself entirely to God so that Christ could be born, the Word made flesh. In this she was the prototype of the church, whose role is to continue to bring Christ to birth in the world, a birth that can only happen through the Spirit. Francis himself called

Mary "the virgin made church."[61] And writing to Clare and her sisters, he addressed them as those who have taken "the Holy Spirit as your spouse."[62] Clare used almost the same words many years later, writing to Agnes of Prague. Mary's example was one of glad obedience, first to the call of God to give birth to the Word; then to Jesus himself, exhorting others to "do whatever he tells you" (John 2:5).

Obedience, then, is the final facet of the jewel. Through intense prayer and contemplation, through listening to visions and prophecy, through the Spirit dwelling within, Francis and Clare came to a clear sense of God's will for them. But there would have been little purpose to all this had they not then put it into practice. Obedience was a natural consequence of all that went before. Once again, Christ was the inspiration and pattern, the one who "emptied himself . . . and became obedient to the point of death—even death on a cross" (Philippians 2:7-8). As by disobedience Adam and Eve had lost their communion with God and their place in paradise, becoming subject to decay and death, so by obedience Christ, through death, came to new life. And he offered this new life to those who would, like him, be obedient to the Father.

This background helps us to understand the stress that Francis, in particular, puts on obedience. It can seem life denying. When some of his brothers asked him what perfect obedience looked like, he gave them the image of the corpse, which has no preferences, does not complain whatever happens to it, and takes no pride in its station. But the context is that of entering into the life of the Son, into the death to which obedience led him, and through that into new and eternal life. Obedience makes sense in the light of the intimacy of the Father and the Son. "My food is to do the will of him who sent me" (John 4:34). As we shall see in the next chapter, Franciscan community life and the obedience necessary to enable that life are founded not in rule but in relationship.

But life giving as it was undoubtedly intended to be, obedience had then, as it has now, a real cost. The ending of the story with which this chapter began illustrates the place of obedience in the life of the early Franciscans.

After a long time in contemplation, Clare and Francis and their companions returned to their meal, and then Clare returned to San Damiano. Her sisters greeted her return with great joy, because they had been worried that Francis might have sent her to another convent. He had already sent Agnes, Clare's sister, to be abbess at Monticelli, at Florence, and had once said to Clare that he might need to send her also to be in charge of a new house. She had replied that she was always ready to go wherever he might send her. The story ends, touchingly, that the sisters rejoiced greatly at discovering that she had not been taken away from them, and that Clare herself was encouraged and consoled by their joy at her return. ॐ

Chapter 4

Brother Sun and Sister Moon

Bonaventure was one of the early Franciscans who did write systematically about prayer. The son of an Italian physician, he was five years old when Francis died in 1226. At the age of twenty-three he joined the Franciscans, and was sent to study in Paris. He became a teacher himself within five years, and at thirty-three became master of the Franciscan school in Paris. At the early age of thirty-six he was elected as minister general of the order, at a critical time in its history. Bonaventure has been called the second founder of the Franciscan order; he was also an eminent theologian. The wider church sought to honor him, first by nominating him as archbishop of York. He refused this offer. Eight years later he was nominated as cardinal and bishop of Albano, and this time the pope insisted that he accept. The story goes that when the pope's messengers arrived at the friary of Mugello near Florence, carrying the red cardinal's hat with its fifteen tassels, Bonaventure, the famous theologian, was washing the dishes. Far from being impressed by this great honor, promotion to one of the highest ranks in the church, he asked them to hang the hat on a tree, and went on doing the dishes.

The matter-of-fact commitment to the mundane realities of life together that Bonaventure showed is another very important mark of Franciscan spirituality, and one that has deep roots in the biblical pictures of God as Creator and Father.

When we think of God as Creator, it is probably the first chapters of Genesis that spring to mind: "In the beginning." The first chapter of Genesis is the well-known story of the seven days of creation, with its regular refrain, "And God saw that it was good." Out of the watery chaos and emptiness God creates all that is—light and darkness; earth, sea, and sky; sun, moon, and stars; plants, animals, and birds; and finally, human beings, made in God's image and likeness. This order of creation reappears in the middle section of Psalm 104, praising God for all that he has made; and in Psalm 8:5-8, there is an echo of making humanity the crown of creation, given mastery over the rest of the created world.

But if we move on to Chapter 2 of Genesis, we find a rather different account of creation. Here the world already exists, and the focus is all on the creation of people, and of people in relationship to each other. This is the other important aspect of God as Creator. God not only creates human beings, but forms them into a people and calls them to enter a covenant relationship with him. The story of the Exodus is central to this picture of God as Creator. He brings the people out of Egypt, through the chaotic waters of the Red Sea, and in the desert forms them into a people to serve him. In the Song of the Sea (Exodus 15:1-18), the waters are almost another adversary along with Pharaoh's army. The word in verse 16b that is translated as "acquired" in NRSV, as "created" (RSV), "purchased" (NJB), or "bought" (NIV), can also be translated as "gotten," and the double meaning of this in terms of both acquiring and begetting is suggestive of God as fathering his people. In another song also ascribed to Moses, God is described as "your father, who created you" (Deuteronomy 32:6), as an eagle caring for its young (Deuteronomy 32:11), as "the God who gave you birth" (Deuteronomy 32:18). In other parts of the Old Testament, too, the people are reminded of their creation (Psalm 95:6-7; Psalm 100:3; Hosea 8:14).

In the New Testament it is perhaps the idea of re-creation that features most strongly. Particularly in Revelation there is a strong emphasis on God creating anew—a new heaven and a new earth (Revelation 21). John here picks up themes from the prophet Isaiah, who blends together all the Old Testament themes of God as Creator. Yahweh is the one who created all things (Isaiah 44:24), who established the earth and defeated chaos (45:18), who formed Israel as a community (43:21), and who is also creating something new (48:6-7). Speaking to a people in exile, the prophet gives them hope. The God who created both their world and them as a people can save them from the new chaos that is engulfing them and re-create them as his people through new and creative deeds.

Paul also uses some of the Old Testament imagery when he writes of Christ as the new Moses, leading God's people to new life through the waters of death in his passion. We share in this re-creating act through our baptism (Romans 6:4; Colossians 2:12).

Both of these aspects of God as Creator—Creator of the world and of a people in covenant with him—play an important role in Franciscan spirituality. Francis' love of creation is the one aspect of his spirituality of which most people are aware, and certainly it was an important element in his way of life. It can provide us with a firm foundation for taking seriously our responsibility for the well-being of creation.

But equally important was Francis' sense that because God had created all things and all people, he was Father of all, and therefore all people and all creation were brother and sister to Francis. His embrace of God as Father is particularly poignant when we remember his rejection of his own father before the bishop, and that there is no evidence that they were ever reconciled.

Relating to God as Father not only affected Francis' prayer life, but also led to characteristically Franciscan ways of leadership, of service, and of relating to one another. Mutuality and equality are favored above hierarchy and power-seeking, and there is an attempt to accept all as given by God, in the same way that families accept their members simply because they are family.

Francis' love for creation can easily become the excuse for a rather sentimental way of relating to nature. A thousand statues of Francis surrounded by rabbits, birds, and other representatives of the acceptable, fluffier face of nature give only a limited view of the dynamism of this mainspring of his life. Francis was not sentimental about nature. Once when he was lodging at a monastery, a sow killed a newborn lamb. When Francis heard of this, he mourned over the lamb, but cursed the pig as evil. The sow immediately became ill and after three days died. As we have seen, Francis told his brothers to eat what was set in front of them as they traveled, and this would certainly have included meat.

He loved creation not just because of its beauty, but because he loved above all the Creator. Bonaventure, writing about Francis' love of Christ, says this:

> Francis sought occasion to love God in everything. ... In everything beautiful, he saw him who is beauty itself, and he followed his Beloved everywhere by his likeness imprinted on creation; of all creation he made a ladder by which he might mount up and embrace Him who is all-desirable.[63]

The word "all" is crucial; as Francis called all creation to praise God, so he saw God's goodness in everything created. He even removed worms from the road, in case they were trodden on. He did, however, have a special devotion for those elements, animals, and birds that he thought reflected some truth about God or faith.

Water reminded him of baptism, and so he threw the water he had used to wash his hands where it would not be trodden on. He walked on rocks reverently, because Christ was called the rock; and had a special love for lambs, because Christ was called the lamb of God. The lark, a small brown bird with a hood, reminded him of his brothers in their brown habits, and he told the brothers to imitate her songs of praise to God and her humility. He once said that if he could speak to the emperor, he would ask him to make a law that on Christmas Day the rich should be obliged to scatter grain for the larks and the other birds, and those who owned an ox or an ass should give them the best fodder. In characteristically extravagant fashion, he wanted even the walls to be smeared with meat on Christmas Day, so that no part of creation should be left out of the celebration.

Ironically, the part of creation that Francis seems to have found hardest to love was his own body. He treated it very harshly for much of his life, perhaps thinking that this was necessary because of his indulgence of it during his early years. He often ate and slept little, was forever giving away any warm clothes he possessed, and would roll in the snow or in rose bushes if he felt that temptation was about to overcome him. But toward the end of his life, he did repent of his harshness, and apologized to his body, which he addressed as Brother Ass.

Francis' respect and love of creation seems to have been reciprocated. Toward the end of his life, he developed a disease of the eyes. His doctor wanted to cauterize him, that is to place a hot iron from his jaw up to the eyebrow of the weaker eye. As the iron was being heated in the fire, Francis spoke to the fire, addressing it as "brother," praising it for its nobility and usefulness, and asking it to be gentle to him. Then he blessed the fire with the sign of the cross. The brothers who were with him could not bear to stay any longer and all fled. Francis did not flinch when the iron was applied, and assured the brothers when they returned that he had felt no pain. The doctor was amazed that a man who was so weak could bear this operation. The writer of this story ascribed the miracle to Francis' love, compassion, and respect for God's creatures.

Love, compassion, and respect are qualities conducive to good relationships in any dimension. Relationship is at the heart of this theme of creation and community. With God as Father at the center, Jesus naturally becomes our brother as well as our Lord. Francis rejoiced in this:

> Oh, how glorious it is, how holy and great, to have a Father in heaven! Oh, how holy, consoling, beautiful, and wondrous it is to have such a Spouse! Oh, how holy and how loving, pleasing, humble, peaceful, sweet, lovable, and desirable above all things to have such a Brother and such a Son: our Lord Jesus Christ.[64]

We are sons and daughters of the Father, we are espoused to Christ, who is also our brother, and whose mother we can be. Clare also uses these images, addressing Agnes as "the spouse and the mother and the sister of my Lord Jesus Christ.'"[65]

The Song of Solomon (Song of Songs) is the main biblical source for the picture of the faithful soul as married to Christ, and Clare draws on this idea throughout her letters to Agnes. In the fourth letter, she quotes directly from the Song of Solomon, and often addresses Agnes as the spouse of Christ. This has a particular resonance here, because Agnes could have married the Emperor Frederick II. In her first letter, Clare says:

> For, though You, more than others, could have enjoyed the magnificence and honor and dignity of the world, and could have been married to the illustrious Caesar with splendor befitting You and His excellency, You have rejected all these things

and have chosen with Your whole heart and soul a
life of holy poverty and destitution. Thus You took
a spouse of a more noble lineage . . . the Lord Jesus
Christ.[66]

Francis' images, too, can all be found in the Bible. Jesus
of course speaks constantly of God as Father—at the age of
twelve, found by his anxious parents in the temple and asking,
"Did you not know that I must be in my Father's house?" (Luke
2:49); teaching the disciples to pray, "Our Father" (Matthew
6:9); assuring them that "it is your Father's good pleasure to
give you the kingdom" (Luke 12:32) and that "whoever has
seen me has seen the Father" (John 14:9); and finally, praying,
"Father, into your hands I commend my spirit" (Luke 23:46).
Jesus made it clear that this relationship is open also to his disciples: "I am ascending to my Father and your Father" (John
20:17).

Jesus himself extended the language of family relationship
beyond family. When Mary and his brothers came looking for
him, he replied, "Who is my mother, and who are my brothers?" And pointing to his disciples, he said, "Whoever does
the will of my Father in heaven is my brother and sister and
mother" (Matthew 12:48-50).

The relationship of equality implied in being brother and
sister informed the model of community life that Francis and
Clare both lived and commended to their followers. Clare was
particularly radical for her time. In most religious communities
of the day, the abbot or abbess was a powerful figure, rather
remote, often living apart from the other members of the com-

munity in considerably better conditions. But, as we have seen, at San Damiano it was only with great difficulty that Clare was persuaded to become abbess at all, and she remained entirely part of the community. Visitors to San Damiano today are shown the corner of the communal dormitory where she slept, and the record of the canonization process is full of stories of how she humbly served her sisters. Her Rule provided that new members could only be admitted, or debts incurred, with the agreement of all the sisters. Each week a meeting was to be held to discuss the life of the house, and all the sisters from the oldest to the youngest could have their say. The abbess and the other office holders could be removed from their positions at any time by the sisters of the house, acting together. All authority came from the group, and the abbess was the servant of the sisters. In fact she was to be so accessible to them that they could speak to her as "ladies do with their servant."[67]

Francis also provided that those in charge (the guardians and ministers) should be servants of all the brothers. He too cared for the brothers he lived with and did not expect to be treated differently because he was the founder of the community. But a firm structure was needed to hold the brothers together in their itinerant way of life, and so Francis legislated for a rather more hierarchical, less democratic system of authority than the one Clare set up at San Damiano, where the sisters were together constantly and could therefore consult regularly as an entire group. The brothers came together only a few times a year, and as the order grew, these meetings were huge, with several thousand brothers gathering from all over Italy and farther away.

But always Jesus was the model. "I did not come to be served but to serve" (compare Matthew 20:28) introduces a brief admonition by Francis that should give all those in positions of authority pause for thought. Francis instructs them that they should only be as glad about such a position as they would be if given the job of washing their brothers' feet. And if they are more upset about losing such an office than they would be about losing the job of foot-washing, then their souls are in peril. It seems that, for Francis, the key to the right use of authority is neither to seek it out nor cling to it; for Clare, the key is to share it.

But for both, authority is best exercised as service. The words that Francis uses tell their own story. Nowhere does he speak or write of superiors; instead those in positions of responsibility are ministers, custodians, or guardians. In the Earlier Rule we read, "And no one should be called Prior, but all generally should be called Friars Minor [that is, lesser brothers]. And the one should wash the feet of the others."[68] That this made great demands on those given responsibilities can be seen in Francis' "Letter to a Minister." We don't know who the recipient was, but from the letter we know that he was in charge of a province of brothers, was having a lot of trouble from them, and wanted to retire to a hermitage, abandoning such a difficult job. Francis wrote to encourage him to continue, to love those who were making his life difficult, and not to wish for them to be better Christians.

What applied inside the community also applied outside. The brothers who worked outside the community (which, in the early days, was probably most of them) were not to hold powerful positions. They were to be laborers or servants, not treasurers, overseers, administrators, managers, or supervisors. From equality he would have them move to "minority"—to be the lesser ones (compare Luke 22:26), following Christ who was "as one who serves" (Luke 22:27). Far from being in control of others, they were to be dependent on others.

Within the community, too, relationship was central. The sisters at San Damiano, and the brothers in their scattered communities, were not just separate individuals, each pursuing their life of prayer or of preaching and service. They were to treat each other as family: "And wherever the brothers may be together or meet [other] brothers, let them give witness that they are members of one family."[69]

Using very feminine language, Francis uses the picture of a mother caring for her son to describe the kind of care that the brothers are to have for each other. He spells out what this means in terms of behavior: primarily, they are to love not only in word but in deed (1 John 3:18). So they are not to quarrel or become angry with each other. Neither are they to speak about another brother behind his back nor to spread gossip. They should not become obsessed by each other's small faults (easier said than done when living with people one has not chosen as companions), but should stay aware of their own faults and weaknesses. Thus they will not judge each other.

Clare too, in her Rule, warns the sisters to guard against "pride, vainglory, envy, greed, worldly care and anxiety, detraction and murmuring, dissension and division."[70] Both Francis and Clare were very realistic about the difficulties of living together and the daily struggle necessary to preserve "the unity of mutual love, which is the bond of perfection."[71] Thomas of Celano witnesses that such unity did exist at San Damiano. Writing four years after the death of Francis, he says that although there were forty or fifty sisters living together (and San Damiano is not a large place), their mutual love bound their wills together and made them of one mind and spirit.

In this, Clare seems to have led by example. Her sisters testified after her death to her desire to serve. She washed the feet of the sisters who had been out begging, fetched water for those eating to wash their hands, and washed the mattresses of those who were sick. At night she would cover up any who were in danger of suffering from the cold.

She had particular compassion for the sick. The provision she made in her Rule no doubt reflects her own practice. The abbess was to find out what they needed by way of food, other practical needs, or someone to talk to, and to provide it as best she could. And this was not to be done in a routine or cold way, but charitably and kindly. The mutuality of this care was expressed in terms of mother and daughter, and sister and sister: "Each should make known her needs to the other with confidence. For if a mother loves and nourishes her daughter according to the flesh, how much more lovingly must a sister love and nourish her sister according to the Spirit!"[72] Francis too, in the different circumstances of his life, provided for the care of the sick. If a brother fell ill, another brother—or several if necessary—were to stay behind with him, "to serve him as they would wish to be served themselves" (compare Matthew 7:12).[73]

Francis himself cared for those who were sick with great tact and with concern for their individual needs. Once he was staying in a friary with an elderly friar who was very weak and sick. Francis knew that the friar had a longing for grapes, so he went with him to a vineyard, and sitting down near a vine with beautiful bunches of grapes, he began to eat them himself. So the brother was not ashamed to eat them too, and to enjoy the grapes and praise God for them.

But the sick too had responsibilities: Francis begs the sick brother to continue to be thankful to God, accepting health or sickness as God's will. Clare expected the sick sisters to make a positive reply to those who visited them. Their sickness did not exempt them from the daily endeavor to maintain love and unity.

For the brothers, the way in which they were to serve their sick brothers was a reflection of their service to any in need. If all people, and indeed all of creation, were their brothers and sisters, then the gospel call was very clear: "Just as you did it to one of the least of these who are members of my family, you did to me," said Christ (Matthew 25:40). So the sense of familial relationship between God and people, among people, and between people and nature, became a strong imperative to service. In serving each other, they were serving Christ.

That sense of family also informed the relationship between Francis and Clare, and hence between the brothers and sisters and between women and men in general. Clare was always very insistent that there was only one Franciscan family, inspired by the same spirit, and committed to the same poverty. She fought hard after Francis' death to remain closely connected to the friars, at a time when some of them sought, with the approval of the church, to distance themselves from responsibility for the communities of women. Clare made no vows except the vow of obedience made to Francis himself at the very beginning of her religious life. By the rules of religious life of the time, that made her part of his community. In her Rule, she reinforced this sense of unity in one community by promising that both she and her sisters would obey Francis' successors. And Francis himself recognized that Clare and her sisters had been called to the same gospel life as the brothers had. In a short letter, which Clare included in her Rule, Francis promised to care for them as he did for his brothers:

> Since by divine inspiration you have made your-
> selves daughters and servants of the most high King,
> the heavenly Father, and have taken the Holy Spirit
> as your spouse, choosing to live according to the
> perfection of the holy Gospel, I resolve and promise
> for myself and for my brothers always to have that
> same loving care and special solicitude for you as [I
> have] for them.[74]

This promise sometimes came into conflict with Francis' wari-ness of becoming too close to Clare and the sisters, a wariness that reflected his attitude toward women in general. A chapter in his Earlier Rule seems out of keeping with his promise to Clare. In it, he instructs his brothers to "avoid impure glances and associations with women."[75] They were not to travel alone with them, eat out of the same dish, or counsel them. The broth-ers who were priests could hear their confessions but not form a deeper relationship where the women would promise obedi-

ence to the brother. It seems hard, but it is a reflection of the
new religious life being lived by the brothers, one where they
did not have the protection of monastery walls for their way of
life. Church manuals of canon law of the twelfth and thirteenth
centuries describe many of the abuses that Francis forbade; he
was eager to protect both his brothers and the women who
associated with them from scandal. As we have seen, he was
often very hard on his own body. He knew his own frailty and
how he could still be tempted away from his commitment to
"Lady Poverty." When people praised him for his sanctity, near
the end of his life, he would say, "Don't assume that I am safe.
I may still have sons and daughters."

The romantic ideas of knighthood and chivalry that influenced Francis' early life, and his attempts to make a name for
himself in war, also influenced his attitudes toward women.
The songs of the troubadours that he sang with his friends
in the streets of Assisi had an idealized view of women. The
knight lover sought a relationship with a seemingly unattain-
able woman, who was usually his social superior, and always a
model of virtue. It was enough for him if, after many years, she
would only smile at him. One troubadour wrote,

> All my prayers these last twenty years
>   have been answered,
> For this day did not my Lady, so beautiful, so virtuous,
> Not glance pitifully in my direction and smile at me:
> Let my heart rejoice for my long vigil of love is now over
> And let no one sully her high virtue and nobility.[76]

But coupled with this formality and caution went a great respect and affection. When Francis lay dying, it was to a woman that he wrote, asking for a few small things to make his last days more comfortable. This was Lady Jacoba de'Settesoli, a widow and a prominent member of the Third Order, those who followed Francis while remaining with their families and in their own homes. Francis affectionately called her Brother Jacoba. They seem to have had a close relationship, and Francis had stayed with her several times at her home in Rome. Such was their closeness that before the letter had been sent, the Lady Jacoba arrived at the friary, bringing with her everything that Francis had asked for—cloth to make a tunic, a pillow, many candles, and a particular cake he was especially fond of, which she had made for him in Rome. Although women were usually forbidden to enter the friary, she was immediately brought in to Francis' bedside. She stayed with him until he died, when she held his body and wept bitterly. The reality of relationship overcame Francis' caution and mistrust of himself.

Creation, community, relationship—all are summed up in the Canticle of the Creatures, perhaps the best known of all of Francis' writings. Many know it in the form of the hymn "All Creatures of Our God and King," with its repeated refrain of "Praise him, alleluia":

> Most High, all powerful, good Lord,
>   to you be praise, glory, honor and all blessing.
> Only to you, Most High, do they belong,
>   and no one is worthy to call upon your name.
> May you be praised, my Lord, with all your creatures,

especially brother sun,
through whom you lighten the day for us.
He is beautiful and radiant with great splendor;
he signifies you, O Most High.
Be praised, my Lord, for sister moon and the stars;
clear and precious and lovely,
they are formed in heaven.
Be praised, my Lord, for brother wind,
and by air and clouds,
clear skies and all weathers,
by which you give sustenance to your creatures.
Be praised, my Lord, for brother fire,
by whom the night is illumined for us;
he is beautiful and cheerful,
full of power and strength.
Be praised, my Lord, for sister, our mother earth,
who sustains and governs us
and produces diverse fruits
and colored flowers and grass.
Be praised, my Lord, by all those who forgive
for love of you
and who bear weakness and tribulation.
Blessed are those who bear them in peace;
for by you, Most High, they will be crowned.
Be praised, my Lord, for our sister,
the death of the body;
from which no one living is able to flee;
woe to those who are dying in mortal sin.
Blessed are those who are found

doing your most holy will;
for the second death will do them no harm.
Praise and bless my Lord and give him thanks
and serve him with great humility.[77]

"Be praised . . . Be praised . . . Be praised"—the dominant theme is that of so many of Francis' prayers, the praise of God. And once again it is a call to universal praise, for all of creation to praise its Creator. The various parts of creation are personified as brother and sister and mother, and perhaps it is not too far-fetched to see them included in Jesus' words about those who do his will, and who are therefore members of his family (Mark 3:35).

The Canticle of the Creatures was written at a time when the Italian language was gradually developing out of Latin. It is thus written in a dialect, not in the formal language of theology and the church. Dialect was the language of the troubadours, the language of their songs and poems of love. The canticle is a love song, written to be sung. We know that it had a tune, which Francis taught to the brothers. But instead of being a song of love for a woman, as the troubadour songs were, this is a song of love for God. Along with "praise," the other word that recurs is "my": "my Lord." The Creator of all things is also intimately bound up with Francis—and not with Francis alone, but with all created things, with which therefore Francis also has an intimate relationship. Brother Sun, Sister Moon, and Mother Earth are as much part of Francis' family as Lady Clare, Brother Leo, and "Brother Jacoba."

The canticle reflects, too, Francis' sense that all creation points to God. There is much debate over the proper way to translate the word *per.* It can be "for," with a sense of giving thanks for the creation; or it can be "by," with a sense of calling all creation to praise God. But perhaps the best translation is "through" or "with," expressing that call to praise God, but now with a sense also of perceiving God's presence and activity in what he has created. Thus the sun gives us light, beautiful and radiant; the wind and weather give us sustenance; Mother Earth produces fruit and herbs to nourish us. Water is useful to us, and fire lights up our darkness. Perhaps we can also see references to the Trinity, which occur so often in Francis' writings. Certainly wind, water, and fire can all symbolize the Spirit. Perhaps the Sun is also the Son? And God the Father, the Creator, is implicit in the entire canticle.

Whatever the deeper meanings that may be discovered in the canticle, it is a marvelous summary of Francis' relationship with the created world, a relationship founded on the discovery of God as his Father, and not his alone but everyone's. In the working out of the implications of this discovery, there is a rich vein for a spirituality of relationship, relationship that binds together all people and all creation into one family of mutual love, respect, and service. ✺

Chapter 5

As Sorrowful, yet Always Rejoicing

The Canticle of the Creatures is so rapturous a prayer that it is easy to imagine it pouring out of Francis in the joyous early days of his conversion. As he roamed the Umbrian hills around Assisi, intoxicated with God, and reveling in his new appreciation of the gifts of the Creator, we can easily imagine him bursting into this song.

But the reality is very different. The canticle was, in fact, written near the end of Francis' life. He had become so identified with Christ that, after a long retreat on Mount La Verna, he had received the stigmata, the marks of Christ's passion in his own body. The wounds of the nails in his hands and feet and the mark of the spear in his side caused him constant pain for the last two years of his life. After La Verna, he went to a leper colony, and then spent the winter preaching, especially on the mystery of Christ crucified. By the spring he was ill, and returned to Assisi, where he stayed in a small hut outside San Damiano. His eye condition had deteriorated, and he had to remain in darkness, unable to bear the light. His sleep was interrupted by field mice running around and even over him.

After fifty days of these conditions, it is not surprising that Francis was feeling sorry for himself, tempted to despair and to doubt God's love. As ever, he turned to prayer, asking Christ to strengthen him. Then he heard a voice asking him, "If the whole earth was changed into gold, the pebbles into precious stones, and the waters into perfumes, and this immense treasure was given you in return for your suffering and trouble, would you not rejoice?"

"I would indeed be happy beyond measure," replied Francis.

"Well," the Lord replied, "because of your patience in trouble you will inherit my kingdom, a far greater treasure."

In the morning, Francis shared this vision with his companions, and then wrote the first eight verses of the canticle—a call to praise God for all his gifts—at a time when Francis could reasonably have felt that he had little for which to thank God. In addition to his own sufferings from sickness, he was also dismayed at the way many of his brothers were living. As the order grew, the life of the brothers became more like the life in the monasteries, with property and learning, and the beginnings of a more settled life. Francis had given up the leadership of the community in his desire to be humble and little; he had cause to feel betrayed by those to whom he had entrusted it. Perhaps he could have echoed Paul's words to the Galatians: "I am astonished that you are so quickly deserting the one who called you in the grace of Christ" (Galatians 1:6).

But Francis had reason to believe that God could bring good out of evil, joy out of suffering. Such reversals had been a part of his life from the beginning of his conversion. His life was marked by a willing embrace of beliefs and actions that were generally considered negative and undesirable. He served lepers, chose poverty, identified deeply with the passion of Christ, accepted both physical and mental suffering, and both practiced and preached penance. It isn't a job description likely to draw many applicants. But far from becoming morose or miserable, Francis was known for his joy.

However, joyfulness was something he had to work at, and a story from the early days shows us the process. At the time when he was being drawn into a deeper life of prayer, he began to be haunted by the image of a woman in Assisi who was known to all the people. She was hunchbacked, and "a hideous sight to all."[78] Francis became obsessed with the fear that he would become like her if he continued in the way of prayer and penance that he was beginning to embrace. In his fear, he heard God within: "Francis, what you have loved vainly in the flesh you should now exchange for things of the spirit, taking the bitter for the sweet."[79] It was shortly after this that Francis met the leper and took another important step on the road of his conversion. Writing about this meeting shortly before he died, he uses the same image of bitter and sweet, showing how deeply he had been affected by these words of God:

> While I was in sin, it seemed very bitter to me to see lepers. And the Lord Himself led me among them and I had mercy upon them. And when I left them, that which seemed bitter to me was changed into sweetness of soul and body; and afterward I lingered a little and left the world.[80]

It was an important lesson. The first rapture of conversion, when God seemed all sweetness, was tempered by temptation, doubt, and fear. But in embracing these unpleasant realities as he embraced the leper, the bitterness was changed into sweetness.

Francis was a realist; he recognized that the way to this transformation often led through ways that went counter to natural human desires and instincts. In both of his "Letters to the Faithful" he acknowledged that "it is sweet to the body to commit sin and it is bitter for it to serve God."[81] But the true sweetness comes in serving God, in being among those who wish to "taste and see that the LORD is good" (Psalm 34:8). Francis changed this quotation to "how sweet the Lord is."[82] There may also be echoes in this image of the call of John the Evangelist (Revelation 10:8-11), which itself draws on the call of Ezekiel (Ezekiel 2:8–3:3).

This willingness to embrace both the bitter and the sweet from God's hand found its fullest expression in the stigmata. It is one of the more difficult parts of Francis' story for many people. Most of us tend to shy away from such an intense identification with the crucifixion. We may even suspect hysteria.

But the early writers on Francis put this extraordinary event firmly in the context of his love for God and desire to do his will, and in this setting it makes sense. The story begins with an unusual gift. In 1213 Count Orlando Chiusi gave Francis a mountain—Mount La Verna—in Tuscany. For the rest of his life, Francis used it as a place of prayer and retreat, and so it was that in August 1224 he retired there with a few companions for forty days of prayer. As he prayed, he was moved to take the book of the gospels and ask God to use it to show him the way ahead. Three times he opened it, and three times it showed him the passion of Christ. Then he understood that his way to God was the way of the cross.

On September 14, the feast of the Holy Cross, Francis prayed for two graces—one that he might feel in his soul and body the pain and grief of the passion; the other that he might feel in his heart the love that compelled Christ to suffer so for sinners. Believing that God would answer his prayer, he set himself to contemplate the passion of Christ and his great love. Then in his prayer he saw a six-winged seraph (compare Isaiah 6:2), beautiful and glorious, nailed to a cross. The sight filled him with wonder and perplexity. In the seraph he saw Christ looking at him kindly and graciously, and so rejoiced. But he also felt great compassion for his being crucified, and so was sorrowful. Celano says, "And so he arose . . . sorrowful and joyful, and joy and grief were in him alternately."[83]

While he sought to understand the vision, an even stranger thing happened. The marks of the nails and the spear that he had seen in the seraph began to appear in his own body. From now until his death two years later, he was never without pain from these wounds, wounds that reflected his intense identification with the crucified Christ. It was as if the love and compassion in his heart could not be contained there, but spilled over into his body, making love visible. Celano says that "the fountain of enlightened love that filled his whole being bubbled forth outwardly."[84] He was speaking of Francis' words, but perhaps this image also helps to explain the stigmata.

This identification with Christ is the main theme of all that the early writers say about the stigmata. Celano calls Francis "this crucified servant of the crucified Lord"[85] and writes of how "true love for Christ had transformed this lover into the very image of Christ."[86] Bonaventure stresses the preeminence of the transformation of the spirit over the more apparently dramatic sign of the physical stigmata: "It was set before his eyes that, as Christ's lover, he might know he was to resemble Christ crucified not by physical martyrdom, but by the fervor of his spirit."[87]

Francis himself took great care not to let even his closest companions see the stigmata. He always kept his hands and feet covered, and was distressed if by accident they were seen. He did not want to be glorified by others because of this gift. On Mount La Verna, earlier in his retreat, he had prayed, "Who are you, my sweetest God, and what am I, your worthless servant?" This sense of the majesty of God and his own littleness stayed with him to the end. With Paul and many others he could say, "May I never boast of anything except the cross of our Lord Jesus Christ, by which the world has been crucified to me, and I to the world" (Galatians 6:14). But there were few who could also go on to say for themselves, "From now on, let no one make trouble for me; for I carry the marks of Jesus branded on my body" (Galatians 6:17). In a very literal sense Francis was "always carrying in his body the death of Jesus, so that the life of Jesus might also be made visible in his body" (compare 2 Corinthians 4:10).

Bonaventure saw Francis' whole life as characterized by encounters with the cross and with the crucified Christ. Addressing Francis after the stigmata, he writes in his biography of the saint:

The very first vision you saw has now been fulfilled; it was revealed to you then that you were to be a captain in Christ's army and that you should bear arms which were emblazoned with the sign of the cross. At the beginning of your religious life the sight of the Crucified pierced your soul with a sword of compassionate sorrow. There can be no doubt that you heard Christ's voice from the cross, which seemed to come from his throne in his sanctuary on high, because we have your own word for it. . . . At the outset of your religious life Christ's Cross was put before you and you took it up and carried it always by living blamelessly, giving others an example to follow.[88]

The example of Christ's self-giving love and trust in God, was one that Francis wanted to keep before him every day. One way he did this was to add to each of the daily services of prayer an additional psalm, which he had composed himself, taking Scripture verses mainly from the psalms. Francis' intention was to compose prayers that Christ himself could have used at various stages of his passion. In praying them daily, he entered more and more deeply into the mystery of the cross, which is the mystery at the heart of the Christian faith. As the entire structure of each of the four gospels leads up to their accounts of the passion—and the whole gospel makes sense only in the light of the passion, death, and resurrection of Christ—so Francis' life of devotion and service was shaped by and revolved around the cross.

Always he was deeply moved by the cross. After the crucifix at San Damiano had spoken to him, three of his early brothers, in a biography published twenty years after Francis' death, record, "From that hour his heart was stricken and wounded with melting love and compassion for the passion of Christ; and for the rest of his life he carried in it the wounds of the Lord Jesus."[89]

Often this compassion overflowed in tears and lamentation. One day, near St. Mary of the Angels, this love for the passion overtook him to such an extent that a passer-by asked if he was ill. But Francis replied that he was weeping for the passion of his Lord, and that he would not be ashamed to go through the whole world weeping for his sake. This so moved the passer-by that he too began to cry and lament.

Even in a psalm he composed for the Christmas season—a joyful celebration of the birth of Christ—he ended with the words, "Offer your bodies and take up your cross; follow his most holy commands to the end."[90] Incidentally, this psalm also illustrates the saint's encyclopedic knowledge of the Bible. In thirteen verses, Francis quotes seven different psalms, reflects on Isaiah's prophecy of the birth of the Messiah (Isaiah 9:6), and uses three quotations from Luke's gospel and one from the first letter of Peter.

But Christ's passion was not simply a subject for meditation and prayer. Francis constantly called his brothers to obey Christ's injunction: "If any want to become my followers, let them deny themselves and take up their cross and follow me. For those who want to save their life will lose it, and those who lose their life for my sake will find it" (Matthew 16:24-25).

The cross was not simply to be an object of devotion, moving his brothers to a deeper love of Christ, but the pattern that should mark their lives. The self-offering of Christ was to be theirs also, and would lead them, like Christ, to suffering and to death, but also to new life. This was not always physical suffering and death—though for some it was—but the suffering of death to self, of poverty, of celibate chastity, of the death to the will implied in obedience.

Clare, too, followed this pattern. Her sisters witnessed to it. One remembered that Clare "instructed her to always have the Lord's passion in her memory."[91] Another recalled that she had a particular devotion to praying the Office of Sext, said at the sixth hour (around midday), because it commemorated the time when Christ was nailed to the cross. Thomas of Celano writes that she also used the Office of the Passion that Francis had composed, and that she recited it with the same affection as Francis himself.

Even the pope recognized that Clare's life was entirely given to Christ crucified. Once, when he came to San Damiano to talk with her, she asked him to bless the bread for their meal. But instead he asked her to make on the loaves the sign of the cross, to which, he added, "you have entirely given yourself." Clare demurred, and only agreed when the pope commanded her under obedience. As she blessed them, the sign of the cross appeared on each loaf. When healing the sick, she also always used the sign of the cross, which both made holy and made whole.

The form of the cross used by Francis, the *tau*, or T-shaped cross, leads naturally to thoughts of repentance and sorrow for sin. It stems from Ezekiel 9:4, where, in the prophet's vision, a scribe is ordered to put a mark on the forehead of those who lament the sins of Jerusalem, so that they will be spared in the slaughter that is about to come. The Hebrew word for "mark" is the last letter of the Hebrew alphabet, *taw*. Hence this form of the cross came to be associated with those who, through repentance, came to salvation.

For both Francis and Clare, the cross, the passion of Christ, called for a response. If God had done so much for them, how could they not seek to return something to him? Penance was, for them, this response, and was therefore central to their lives. In fact, at first Francis and his companions were called "the penitent men of Assisi."[92] Somewhat like the stigmata, this is an idea that can make us uneasy. It too easily smacks of self-hatred, of groveling before God, of describing ourselves as "miserable sinners."

But for Francis, penance flowed from his devotion to God and his daily recognition of God's generosity. Penance was the starting point of his Testament, and was itself a gift from God: "The Lord granted me, Brother Francis, to begin to do penance."[93] Why did he need to do penance? Because he was "in sin." Sin was not just an occasional act, but a state, the state of fallen humanity, characterized by bitterness. But then for Francis, as for humanity as a whole, God intervened. Just as at Nazareth and on Calvary God came to the rescue of those who could not rescue themselves, so it was for Francis. The Lord himself led him among the lepers, who were the focus of the bitterness in his life at that time. When Francis left the lepers, he left as it were by a different road, facing in another direction.

God had turned him around, and in the process turned what was bitter into sweetness. This is a very good description of what the New Testament word *metanoia*, usually translated as "repentance," really means (compare Mark 1:4, 15; 6:12; Luke 15:7; Romans 2:4; Revelation 2:5). At root it is about turning around.

Francis always uses the phrase "doing penance" where others might talk about conversion. So in preaching penance, as he often did, he was calling his hearers not just to sorrow for their sins, though that was very important, but also to conversion, to turning, to a complete reversal of values, which would make what had been bitter sweet.

The early Christians were called those who "have been turning the world upside down" (Acts 17:6). Francis and his followers could well have been called the same, but as with the early Christians this was only because they had themselves been turned around, and turned upside down in their values.

In Francis and his brothers we see lived out the upside-down world of the beatitudes, where all the unlikely people are blessed—the poor, the hungry, the mourners, the meek, the persecuted. But they are the ones to whom Jesus promised the kingdom of heaven and the vision of God (Matthew 5:3-12; Luke 6:20-23). Francis lived out these radically reversed values, and his preaching of penance was part of that.

In fact Francis echoed the beatitudes in part of his Earlier Rule, where he provided a model homily or exhortation, which any of the brothers could use as they wished. The message he gave them to share can be summed up in two words—"praise" and "penance." The model begins with praise of God, the

Holy Trinity. Then it exhorts listeners to do penance in ways that will bring forth fruit in their relations with each other, reminds them that God's forgiveness of them depended on their own willingness to forgive (Matthew 6:14-15; compare Mark 11:25-26; Luke 6:37), and encourages them (in line with one of the decrees of the Fourth Lateran Council) to make their confession. Then Francis goes on, "Blessed are those who die in penance, for they shall be in the kingdom of heaven."[94] And the end reflects the turning implicit in any true penance—not just "Beware of and abstain from every evil . . ." but ". . . persevere in good till the end."[95]

The simplicity of those words is characteristic of Francis' preaching on penance. It can be clearly seen in a letter believed to have been written to guide the many men and women who were inspired by his life and preaching to join him, but who were prevented by family responsibilities from becoming brothers with Francis or sisters with Clare. Soon they were formed into the Third Order, completing the Franciscan family. In their living out of Franciscan values in everyday life, they complemented the itinerant preaching of the First Order brothers and the enclosed life of prayer of the Second Order sisters. But in the early days the Third Order was known as the Brothers and Sisters of Penance, so much was penance a defining feature of the life to which Francis called them.

Despite this emphasis, he sets out no complicated program of penitential practices and obligations. In the first half of the letter, addressed to "those who do penance," only a few simple, though demanding, things are asked of them—love of God with the whole of their being, love of neighbor, turning away from sin and vice, receiving the Eucharist, and being fruitful. As always with Francis, action is called for—living a life, not simply consenting to ideas. But the reward is great: "Oh, how happy and blessed are these men and women when they do these things and persevere in doing them, since the Spirit of the Lord will rest upon them and he will make his home and dwelling among them."[96] Penance restores relationship with God, the relationship broken by sin (Genesis 3), and makes us children of the Father (Matthew 5:45), and spouses, brothers, and mothers of Christ (Matthew 12:50). The rest of this chapter is a glowing celebration of a life restored to the richness of relationship with God.

The second half of the letter, addressed to "those who do not do penance," has a very different flavor. Such people are blind, deceived, lacking in wisdom. Death is not even mentioned in the first part; it is irrelevant for those who have already "passed from death to life" (1 John 3:14). But much of the second section is given to a vivid description of dying in sin, dying a bitter death. Everything that the dying people possess is lost, and their families and friends curse them for not having made more wealth to leave to them. The children of the devil (compare John 8:44) go to be with him for eternity. The wages of sin are indeed death. But penance is a remedy for sin, because penance is a way of sharing in the cross, the only ultimate remedy for sin.

So in a paradoxical way, penance becomes a cause for joy. Though the medicine may be bitter, the end, which is life and health and wholeness, is sweet and to be desired.

Some of Francis' contemporaries thought that he and his

brothers did too much penance and had become unbalanced because of it. And there are stories that seem to give good cause for this belief.

One day, Francis told Brother Ruffino to go and preach in Assisi. Ruffino, claiming to be simple and stupid and without the gifts necessary for preaching, asked not to be sent, but Francis commanded him under obedience to go. And what was more, he told him to go dressed only in his breeches, because he had not obeyed immediately. So Ruffino took off his habit and set off. When he arrived in the church and began to preach, the people laughed at him, saying, "These men do so much penance that they have become fools, and out of their minds." Meanwhile Francis was having second thoughts. Ruffino had been one of the greatest gentlemen in Assisi before joining the brothers; how dare he order him to humiliate himself in such a way? So Francis too stripped off his habit and went to join Ruffino. And the people laughed at him too. Ruffino had been preaching about repentance and penance, and Francis took up the theme with such eloquence that the laughter of the people turned to tears. Throughout all Assisi, says the writer of the Little Flowers, such weeping and mourning for the passion of Christ had never been seen. Then Francis and Ruffino put on their habits again and returned home, praising and glorifying God.

It is hard to see humiliation in anything but a negative light, but the root of the word is the same as that of "humble" and "humility." It comes from the same word as "humus" and has a sense of sharing in the condition of the earth, which is simply there to be used, to be trodden underfoot. Again this is a difficult concept today, when self-worth is rightly seen to be important. Francis' stress on humility, on his own littleness and nothingness, can easily seem psychologically unhealthy and spiritually unhelpful. But Murray Bodo explains it well:

> This nothingness or littleness is a theological state-ment and not, as we moderns sometimes think, a psychological one. Francis is not looking down upon himself or demeaning himself or looking at himself at all. He is looking at God and simply stating what for him is a fact: God is God and Francis is not a god. This perspective will color everything he is to become and everything he will do.[97]

This littleness is the condition in the Bible of the very poor, those who cannot be self-sufficient but who must rely on the help of others and ultimately on the help of God, for their very survival. It is the condition of Mary, rejoicing in the Magnifi-cat that God has "looked with favor on the lowliness of his servant" (Luke 1:48). It is the condition of the meek, who will inherit the earth (Matthew 5:5).

It is the condition of those who know that they cannot and do not need to earn God's grace, forgiveness, and love, but that these are gifts freely given. From this perspective, humil-ity is closely linked to joy, and Francis often responded with joy to an opportunity to recognize God's greatness and his own littleness.

His close friend Masseo wanted to test his humility one day, and so asked him, "Why does all the world run after you, want to see and hear you, and obey you? You are not handsome, or noble, or highly educated. Why after you?" Francis was filled with joy and caught up to God. Finally he answered Masseo, "Because God has chosen me, great sinner though I am, to show that all virtue and all goodness belong to him, and that anyone who glories should glory in the Lord." Then Masseo knew that Francis was indeed firmly rooted in humility.

It was characteristic of Francis to be joyful and to give thanks. But his joy and gratitude were always grounded in an awareness of sinfulness and of human fallenness. In fact, this awareness seemed to increase his joy—God gave so much, not to those who deserved it, but to the self-centered and sinful. God's mercy was unbounded, and this was always a cause for thanksgiving.

This unbounded mercy is also a model for us to follow. As we have seen, Francis wrote a short but moving letter to one of his brothers, who as minister was responsible for one of the provinces of the friars. He was finding the work very demanding—especially dealing with the brothers who sinned—and wanted to retire to a hermitage. Francis asked him to see everything as grace, and in a challenging sentence for any whose lives are not as they would choose, wrote, "And you should desire that things be this way and not otherwise."[98] The minister should show God's mercy to the brothers who sin, the mercy that goes beyond what is asked, and certainly beyond what is deserved:

> There should not be any brother in the world who
> has sinned, however much he may possibly have
> sinned, who, after he has looked into your eyes,

> would go away without having received your mercy,
> if he is looking for mercy. And if he were not to seek
> mercy, you should ask him if he wants mercy.[99]

Authority is to be exercised in relationships, looking into each other's eyes. Outdoing even Jesus' command to forgive "seventy times seven" (Matthew 18:22), Francis tells the minister that even if the brother sins a thousand times "before your very eyes,"[100] he is to love him still, so that he can be drawn back to God.

God's unbounded love, sufficient to draw back the sinner, is also cause for joy in sickness. Francis begs brothers who are sick to give thanks to their Creator for everything, and to will only what God wants for them, whether that is sickness or health. Clare lived out this exhortation. She was ill for twenty-eight years of her life at San Damiano, and often confined to bed. She never used her illness as an excuse to avoid prayer, and would be propped up in bed so that she could spin thread and make altar linen for the churches around Assisi. But she never complained, and she always turned away from herself to care for others, to praise God, and to give thanks for his gifts.

Even as she lay dying, she trusted and praised God: "Go calmly in peace, for you will have a good escort, because he who created you has sent you the Holy Spirit and has always guarded you as a mother does her child who loves her. O Lord, may You Who have created me, be blessed."[101]

For Paul, death was "the last enemy" (1 Corinthians 15:26). For Francis, death was sister, and included in the Canticle of the Creatures as both cause and means of thanksgiving to God.

Both Francis and Clare spent their last days in blessing those they were leaving. Francis "spent the few days that remained before his death in praise, teaching his companions whom he loved so much to praise Christ with him . . . He exhorted death itself, terrible and hateful to all, to give praise, and going joyfully to meet it, he invited it to make its lodging with him. "Welcome," he said, "my sister death."[102]

That ability to welcome whatever happens as a gift of God, however unlikely that may seem, leads to joy. It is the attitude behind one of the most paradoxical and characteristic of all Franciscan stories, the story of perfect joy.

One day, Francis and Leo were walking together from Perugia to St. Mary of the Angels, a distance of about six miles. It was winter, and bitterly cold. As they struggled on together, Francis began to speak. "Brother Leo," he said, "if the brothers here set a marvelous example of holiness, write it down that this is not perfect joy." A little further on, he said, "Brother Leo, if the brothers restore sight to the blind, hearing to the deaf and speech to the dumb, if they make the lame and the paralyzed walk, and cast out demons, and even if they bring the dead back to life, write that this is not perfect joy." Yet a little further, and Francis spoke again: "Brother Leo, if the brothers had all the knowledge possible, of languages and sciences and Scripture, and could prophesy the future and reveal the secrets of people's consciences and their souls, write that this is not perfect joy." For the fourth time, Francis spoke: "Brother Leo, even if the brothers could speak with the tongues of angels, and knew all there is to know about creation—the courses of the stars, the healing powers of herbs, the powers of animals, trees, stones, water, write that this is not perfect joy." And again, "Brother Leo, even if the brothers should preach so convincingly that all the non-Christians in the world are converted to Christ, write that this is not perfect joy."

Finally, Brother Leo replied, "So tell me, where is perfect joy to be found?"

And Francis said, "If we arrive at St. Mary of the Angels, wet through, frozen, covered with mud, tired and hungry, and we knock at the door, and the porter comes and asks angrily, "Who are you?" and we tell him that we are two of his brothers, but he does not believe us but locks the door against us, leaving us in the snow and the wind—If we bear this patiently and humbly, without complaint, then this would be perfect joy. And if we continue to knock, and he becomes angry and comes out to drive us away, calling us vile thieves, and we bear this too with patience and with joy, then this would be perfect joy. And if we come again, begging him to let us in, and he drives us away with blows, rolling us in the snow, and we bear this too with patience and joy, thinking of the passion of Christ, then this would be perfect joy. For above all the gifts of the Holy Spirit which Christ gives is the gift of suffering for his love. We cannot glory in any other gift of God, because they are not ours. As St. Paul says, 'What do you have that you did not receive? And if you received it, why do you boast as if it were not a gift?' (1 Corinthians 4:7). But we may glory in the cross of trials and afflictions, for they are ours. . . . Far be it from me to glory except in the cross of our Lord Jesus Christ" (Galatians 6:14, RSV). ✺

Chapter 6

As Poor, yet Making Many Rich

After the death of Francis, Clare became in many ways the holder of his vision for the whole Franciscan movement. She had a particular and passionate concern to maintain the poverty that had been at the heart of his vision. The church was always rather uneasy about this Franciscan value, especially for women's communities. When Pope Gregory IX (who, as Cardinal Hugolino, had been a close friend and supporter of Francis) came to Assisi for Francis' canonization, less than two years after his death, he also visited Clare at San Damiano. Here, he tried to persuade her to receive possessions, because of the dangerous and difficult times in which they lived. But Clare resisted strongly. She was bound by a vow of poverty and had no desire to be free of it. As we have seen, when the pope offered to absolve her from her vow, if that was all that stood in her way, she replied, "Absolve me from my sins, but do not absolve me from following Christ." She was a young woman, little more than thirty, and untrained theologically, yet she stood up to the head of the entire church in asserting the centrality of poverty in following Christ.

And this was not an isolated incident. From the very early days of her religious life, poverty had been for Clare, as for Francis, absolutely essential—and not just personal poverty, but corporate. If personal poverty alone had been enough, Clare could have stayed as a servant at the Benedictine monastery of San Paolo to which Francis first took her. But the monastery itself was rich, and that did not satisfy Clare.

Life at San Damiano was very different. Food was often scarce. One of the miracles reported in Clare's canonization process tells of a day when there was only half a loaf of bread to feed fifty sisters. Clare told Sister Cecilia to cut fifty slices from it, and she not unreasonably replied that the miracle of the loaves and fishes would be needed to get fifty slices out of that. But obediently she began to cut, and produced fifty "large and good" slices.

The building too left something to be desired. In 1246, as a well-established monastery with many sisters, it was in so bad a state of repair that the main door fell on top of Clare while she was closing it.

So important was poverty to her that in 1215, only three years after her arrival at San Damiano, she sought and obtained from Pope Innocent III the unprecedented "Privilege of Poverty"—the right to live without possessions or endowments. After her encounter with Pope Gregory in 1228, she sought written confirmation of this privilege, presumably fearing that this Pope might overturn the decision of his predecessor. But Gregory did confirm what Innocent III had given, and for the time being Clare could relax. In some ways this was surprising, because Gregory (as Cardinal Hugolino) had given Clare and her sisters a Rule some ten years before that was based largely on the Rule of St. Benedict, and hence did not contain the intense poverty to which they were committed. The struggle continued until the end of Clare's life. Another pope, Innocent IV, provided another new Rule in 1247, and this one allowed common ownership of goods, and a procurator (an agent from outside the monastery) to handle their financial affairs. Clare began to write her own Rule, which was approved in 1252 by Cardinal Raynaldus, the Protector of the order. But Clare was not satisfied until it had been approved by Innocent IV. This happened on August 9, 1253. Two days later, Clare died.

This brief excursion into history shows both Clare's determination to keep faith with Francis and the church's suspicion and unwillingness to authorize such an unprecedented way of life. Perhaps officials were made wary by the existence of a number of radical and unauthorized groups in the church who followed the slogan "poor, to follow the Christ who was poor on earth." As we saw in Chapter 1, these included some who tipped over into heresy. The pursuit of poverty could be a dangerous one.

But that slogan contains the kernel of why poverty was so central for Francis and Clare. It was at the heart of following Christ, who "though he was rich, yet for your sakes he became poor, so that by his poverty you might become rich" (2 Corinthians 8:9).

It was this example of Christ that inspired both Francis and Clare. It was to Christ and to his mother that Francis looked when, just before his death, he wrote to Clare and to her sisters,

> I, brother Francis, the little one, wish to follow the life and poverty of our most high Lord Jesus Christ

and of His most holy mother and to persevere in this until the end; and I ask and counsel you, my ladies, to live always in this most holy life and in poverty.[103]

Clare set these words at the heart of her Rule. Not only is the call to poverty the sixth chapter of the twelve that make up the Rule, but in the original parchment it is placed in the middle, which was traditionally the place for the most important part of a document.

In her Testament, too, poverty has the central place, poverty of which Christ was the inspiration and Francis the prime example: "The Son of God never wished to abandon this holy poverty while He lived in the world, and our most blessed Father Francis, following His footprints, never departed, either in example or teaching, from this holy poverty."[104] She saw Christ as having embraced poverty throughout his life: "poor as He lay in the crib, poor as He lived in the world, Who remained naked on the cross."[105] In this she was a good pupil of Francis. In his writings he often quoted from 2 Corinthians 8:9 (for example, in the "Second Letter to the Faithful"): "Though he [Christ] was rich beyond all other things, in this world He, together with the most blessed Virgin, His mother, willed to choose poverty."[106]

Francis saw this choice of poverty by Christ as not simply choosing to live in a particular way, but as entering into a relationship. Poverty was for him a person, Lady Poverty, who was waiting in the cave at Bethlehem to greet Christ when he was born, who walked with him through his life, when he had "nowhere to lay his head" (Matthew 8:20), who stayed with him through his trial when everyone else deserted him, who mounted the cross with him, and was buried with him. The incarnation, when Christ "emptied himself" (Philippians 2:7) was the means by which Christ took poverty as his spouse. But when he was resurrected and returned to heaven, Lady Poverty was left alone and an outcast in the world.

Francis was grieved that Poverty was no longer wanted, and resolved to take her as his bride as Christ had done. Early in his conversion, shortly after his return from Spoleto, he had organized a party for all his friends. After the feast, they were going through the streets singing, when he was touched with such sweetness by God that he could not move or speak. His friends naturally wondered what was wrong with him and teased him, asking if he was in love and planning to get married. "You are right," replied Francis, to their amusement. "I was thinking of wooing the noblest, richest, and most beautiful bride ever seen."[107]

And Celano wrote,

> Looking upon poverty as especially dear to the Son of God, though it was spurned throughout the whole world, he sought to espouse it in perpetual charity. Therefore, after he had become a lover of her beauty, he not only left his father and mother, but even put aside all things, that he might cling to her more closely as his spouse and that they might be two in one spirit.[108]

This can seem a very romantic view of poverty. Poverty as a bride to be married is an idea particular to Francis, but his attitude to poverty and his belief that following Christ meant embracing poverty have good biblical roots. Paul's descriptions of Christ's self-emptying in Philippians 2 and of Christ choosing poverty in 2 Corinthians, are consonant with how Christ lived and what he said. He was born in a stable, his mother a virgin (in the Old Testament a symbol of poverty and barrenness, not purity); he became a refugee in Egypt, lived by the work of his hands as a carpenter, left home to be a traveling preacher, and chose mainly working men to be his companions. He was the focus of much suspicion, was finally betrayed, died naked and alone, and was buried in a borrowed tomb.

How was this Christ-centered poverty to be lived out? What did it mean for Francis to be the spouse of Lady Poverty?

The most obvious way was in relation to money, and Francis did have very firm views about that. He despised money so much, in fact, that he had a physical abhorrence for it. In both of his Rules, he forbade the brothers from receiving, possessing, or even handling coins. They were to think of them as having no more value than stones or dung. When a brother carelessly picked up some coins left as an offering at the Portiuncula (one of the early friaries), Francis ordered him to take them in his mouth and put them on the dung heap outside.

This prohibition has caused endless problems to followers of Francis ever since, and has been the cause of many splits in the Franciscan family. As the order grew, ways were found (with the full approval of the church) of keeping the letter of the Rules while evading the spirit. Money for the brothers to use was held by "spiritual friends"; alternatively, all the possessions of the order were deemed to belong to the church, with the brothers simply having use of them. A small sign of how far the brothers moved away from Francis' vision can be seen in the fact that it was a Franciscan friar, Luca Bartolemeo Pacioli, who in 1494 invented double-entry bookkeeping!

On the other side of the argument, it has also caused problems to those who see Francis' absolute view of poverty as romanticizing or glamorizing it, denying the corroding effects of living daily with not enough, of debt and dependence and the limitations imposed by being poor.

But both of these miss the point. Francis' poverty was chosen. He chose, in love, to marry Lady Poverty and to live his life with her. He found in poverty a way to God. He did not impose it on others and in fact sought to relieve their poverty, not to tell them that they should rejoice in it.

Bonaventure writes, "Francis saw Christ's image in every poor person he met, and he was prepared to give them everything he had, even if he himself had urgent need of it. He even believed that they had a right to such alms, as if they belonged to them."[109] Anything that Francis was given he thought of as belonging to him only until he met someone poorer. It was a gift from God and remained a gift, to be passed on again to someone else as a gift: "God the great Almsgiver will regard it as a theft on my part, if I do not give what I have to someone who needs it more."[110] There is no concept here of deserving and undeserving poor, only of need.

Although money was a particular focus of poverty for Francis, this was largely due to the particular times in which he lived and the meaning that money—coin—had at that time. It was still not universally available, and the poor in particular still lived largely without it. It was a means of accumulating capital, rather than a daily means of exchange. Therefore, to have money was to identify with the rich and the secure, and this was what Francis wanted his brothers and sisters to shun.

The deeper meaning of poverty for Francis is found in looking at the words he used. He never wrote of living *sine rebus mundi*—"without the things of this world," that is, in destitution. Normally when he wrote about poverty, he used the phrase *sine proprio*, which is difficult to translate directly into English. But the central meaning is "without anything of one's own," without appropriating anything to oneself. Poverty is about possessing, rather than about possessions.

Material poverty was the beginning, not the end, for Francis. He was often inconsistent in his Rules and other writings about precisely what this should mean for his brothers. On the one hand, he insisted that those joining the community must give away all that they possessed; on the other he allowed the brothers to have breviaries, which were a luxury item, written individually by hand on parchment. Sometimes he insisted that the brothers must own no property, have no house or church of their own; at other times he asked them to open their houses to everyone, and to beautify their churches with precious items. Material poverty was, it seems, not an absolute value, to be guaranteed by legislation, but a sign of a deeper inner state. It was sacramental—an outward sign of an inner reality—and sacramental too in helping those who embraced it to move toward that inner reality, to let go of all that kept them from God.

But it was the deeper levels of poverty that really concerned Francis. In the Admonitions, probably delivered by Francis to gatherings of his brothers, we can identify three areas where Franciscan poverty challenged them and still challenges us to live *sine proprio,* without anything of our own.

The first is in relation to ourselves. In Admonition 5 Francis lists some of the things to which we cling for our identity, for our sense of ourselves. They include knowledge, good looks, wealth, and spiritual gifts—a pretty comprehensive list. But, says Francis, you cannot glory in these things, you cannot take the credit for them, because they are not in reality yours. They are all gifts from God.

Our religion, too, can be a snare. In Admonition 6 Francis asks us to imitate the "sheep of the Lord," who followed the good shepherd through all the trials of his life and death, and who have therefore received eternal life. It is not enough simply to know about, to admire, to tell others such things—that is to appropriate what is not ours. Francis' warning is stark: "Therefore, it is a great shame for us, servants of God, that while the saints [actually] did such things, we wish to receive glory and honor by [merely] recounting their deeds."[111] He gives the same warning about Scripture—it is death simply to seek knowledge of Scripture in order to be praised as wise, and not to live in the spirit of the words. Gifts and abilities, religious tradition and knowledge—all can lead us astray if we see them as our possessions.

Deeper still is the poverty of letting go of our good name and our reputation. In Admonition 14 Francis interprets the first beatitude: "Blessed are the poor in spirit, for theirs is the kingdom of heaven" (Matthew 5:3). We may build up a reputation for ourselves through the quality of our spiritual lives—our prayer, abstinence, good works. But this too can lead us away from real poverty if it becomes something to which we cling. If we become upset when others say negative things about us, then we are still clinging to something, still saying "mine," and are not truly poor in spirit.

This leads us to the second level of poverty that Francis identifies, that of relations with others. Admonition 11 appears at first sight to have nothing to do with poverty. It deals with the brothers' response to those who sin and calls upon them not to be angry or disturbed by the sins of others. Further, it suggests that to become angry or disturbed by anyone is to commit sin, because it usurps what rightly belongs to God. It is easy to cling to our anger or resentment, to justify our feelings on the grounds of what has been done to us by others, and, in a sense, to hoard and treasure up our hurt feelings. Envy too must be shunned. To envy the good that another has is to envy God, because God is the giver of all good.

But deeper than all of these feelings is the will, the most prized of our possessions but also the root of the primal sin. In the garden of Eden Adam was offered freely the fruit of every tree except the tree of the knowledge of good and evil (Genesis 2:16-17). By choosing to disobey God's command and exalting his own will over God's will, Adam became the archetype of all sinfulness. "For," Francis writes, "the person eats of the tree of the knowledge of good who appropriates to himself his own will and thus exalts himself over the good things which the Lord says and does in him."[112] Dispossession of the will in obedience to others is thus both a deep expression of poverty and the most sure remedy for sin. Thus Jesus' words, "None of you can become my disciple if you do not give up all your possessions" (Luke 14:33), take on a meaning far beyond that of giving up material possessions. They will affect how we relate to those in authority over us and to our own exercise of authority. Those in authority must exercise it in a spirit of poverty, not clinging to their position or viewing themselves as more important than the brothers given the job of washing the feet of the others. In fact, they should positively desire the humbler job, and those already in humble positions should not wish to be promoted.

Finally, poverty reaches its deepest level in our relationship with God. As we let go of our material possessions, our gifts, our knowledge, our spiritual wisdom and tradition, our good name, our power over others, and our own will, so we come finally to stand before God in simplicity and nakedness, as Francis stood before the bishop in the square of Assisi. As we come to acknowledge everything as gift, we see that we have nothing of our own, except, says Francis, our sin: "And we should be firmly convinced that nothing belongs to us except our vices and sins."[113] The call to poverty is therefore a call to a life of constant conversion, in which we seek ultimately to dispossess ourselves of these too. But this is hard, and goes down deeply to the very roots of our being. We need to practice on something easier, and this is where material poverty and poverty in relation to ourselves and in our relations with others have their part to play.

Paradoxically, this way of stripping and dispossession, of complete poverty, is also a way of immense richness. Acknowledging that we have nothing of our own except our sins, and seeking to let go of those too, leaves us empty, with space to receive in abundance all that God gives. Francis believed that this would work out in very practical ways. He told his brothers that if they embraced poverty they would be provided for. God, he said, had made a contract between the brothers and the world, that they were to set the world a good example, and the world was to provide for their needs.

His faith was fulfilled. Once, when more than five thousand brothers had gathered at the Church of St. Mary of the Angels for a general chapter, they had so little that it was known as the chapter of the mats, because they had only tents made of rush matting to sleep in. But the people from all the towns around Assisi, as well as from Assisi itself, supplied all their needs, coming with carts laden with bread, wine, beans, cheese, and other food, as well as bowls, cups, and cooking pots.

This practical provision is only the lowest expression of a theology of exchange that lies at the heart of Franciscan poverty. It stems from the passage already quoted from 2 Corinthians. Christ became poor, leaving the glory of heaven, dispossessing himself of his power and majesty, in order that we, through following his example, might become rich.

Clare, writing to Agnes, spells it out:

> What a great laudable exchange: to leave the things of time for those of eternity, to choose the things of heaven for the goods of earth, to receive the hundredfold in place of one, and to possess a blessed and eternal life.[114]

She is quoting directly some of the words of Jesus to his disciples: "And everyone who has left houses or brothers or sisters or father or mother or children or fields, for my name's sake, will receive a hundredfold, and will inherit eternal life" (Matthew 19:29). This passage follows immediately after Jesus' words to the rich young man, that if he wishes to be perfect he should sell all his possessions, give the money to the poor, and follow Jesus (a practice followed precisely by Francis' followers and laid down in the Rule), and the dialogue between Jesus and the disciples about its being harder for a rich person to enter heaven than for a camel to go through the eye of a needle (Matthew 19:16-24).

There is a sense of coming full circle: Poverty will lead to the kingdom of heaven, and what is that but a return to the condition of the garden of Eden, before human sin destroyed the perfect harmony of divine and human that God had created? In a meditation on poverty written shortly after Francis' death, an anonymous writer has Lady Poverty speaking of being with Adam and Eve in Eden:

> I was at one time in the paradise of my God where man went naked; in fact I walked in man and with man in his nakedness through the whole of that most splendid paradise, fearing nothing, doubting nothing, and suspecting no evil. . . . I was rejoicing exceedingly and playing before him all the while, for, possessing nothing, he belonged entirely to God.[115]

That is the end point of Franciscan poverty, to be "as having nothing, and yet possessing everything" (2 Corinthians 6:10).

Harry Williams expresses well the joy that comes through this attitude:

> Poverty as a positive quality means the recognition that in the most real sense the world is mine, whoever owns it in the narrow technical sense. Poverty is thus the ability to enjoy the world to the full because I am not anxious about losing a bit of it or acquiring a bit of it. Poverty takes pleasure in a thing because it is, and not because it can be possessed. Poverty is thus able to taste the flavor of life to the full.[116]

Certainly Francis did not intend poverty to be gloomy. "Where there is poverty with joy," he writes in Admonition 27, "there is neither covetousness nor avarice."[117] And in one of the earliest parts of the Earlier Rule, quoting from Philippians 4:4, he asks the brothers to "beware not to appear outwardly sad and like gloomy hypocrites; but let them show that they are joyful in the Lord and cheerful and truly gracious."[118]

If joy is an unexpected companion of poverty, work is rather more expected. The contract with the world that ensured that the needs of the brothers and sisters were provided for did not excuse them from work. And this was to be humble, manual work, the work of the poor. It was characteristic of both the brothers and the sisters that they did their own work, not having lay sisters or brothers, or servants, paid or unpaid, as did many of the older established monasteries. The aim of this work was not to earn wages, or to trade with the goods made, but to avoid idleness and to share the condition of the poor.

The other side of work was begging. It has been said of Clare and her sisters that "they worked to give, and begged to live." Clare's work was spinning, and she made church linen from the cloth produced. Other sisters cultivated the garden at San Damiano. The produce of this work was given away. In order to live, some sisters went out begging, as did the brothers. This was not seen as failure or in any way shameful. Clare wrote in her Rule, "As pilgrims and strangers in this world who serve the Lord in poverty and humility, let them send confidently for alms."[119] Francis had the same matter-of-fact approach: "And when it should be necessary, let them seek alms like other poor people."[120] Thus they trod the fine line between confidence in God's provision and the temptation to sit back in idleness as if the world owed them a living. Other people were one of the means by which God supplied their needs. They were not to be ashamed to make these needs known, to acknowledge that they were not entirely self-reliant.

Finally, peace is, for Franciscans, closely linked to poverty. When the bishop of Assisi said to Francis and his first brothers that it seemed to him very hard that they should possess nothing, Francis replied that if they had possessions, they would need weapons to defend them. Poverty was not only the foundation of the spiritual life for the individual and the community, but also the antidote to war and violence.

Francis lived in violent times, when cities fought each other over territory, and the armies of the great terrorized the cities. Francis told his brothers to use the greeting "God give you peace" to those they met on the road and as they began their sermons, and these were no empty words. They led on to practical peace making, and there are a number of stories of Francis coming into situations of conflict, mediating between the warring parties, and bringing peace. Having, in poverty, nothing to lose himself, and no interest to defend, he could be acceptable to all sides in a quarrel.

This gift of reconciliation extended beyond the simply human into God's wider creation. Once, the people of Gubbio were being terrorized by a ravenous wolf. It used to come into the town and seize not only their livestock but also their children. The people were afraid to go beyond the city walls for fear of meeting the wolf, even though they went out armed. Francis was at this time living in Gubbio, and offered to go out to the wolf, although everyone warned him against such a risk. Francis set out with some companions, though before they came to the wolf's lair, Francis was alone. The wolf came running out, mouth open, but Francis addressed him as "Brother Wolf," made the sign of the cross, and asked him in the name of Christ not to harm anyone. Then he spoke to the wolf, acknowledging that it was hunger that had driven him to violence, and promising that the citizens of Gubbio would feed him if he promised not to harm people or animals in the future. He asked the wolf if he agreed, and the wolf put his right paw into Francis' hand. Then the wolf and Francis went back together to Gubbio, right into the town square. Francis told the people of his agreement with the wolf, and they in their turn promised to feed him daily, sharing what they had with him. Once again, in front of all the people, the wolf signaled his agreement by putting his right paw into Francis' hand. For two years the wolf lived peacefully with the people of Gubbio, going from door to door of the town. The people kept their pledge to feed him, and he harmed no one, and not even the dogs barked at him. When he died of old age, the people grieved. They had lost a reminder of Francis, and a symbol of the reconciliation and peace that he had brought. ❧

Chapter 7

Into All the World

In the mid-1970s, a young woman spent the weekend at a Franciscan friary in a small seaside village in the north of England. Traveling from her parents' home in Scotland to college in Newcastle, she had often seen the village and meant to visit it. When she discovered that there was a house that offered hospitality, it seemed a good opportunity to do it at last. She got more than she bargained for. Over one very cold weekend, without knowing anything about Francis and Clare, she became hooked on the Franciscan way. It was something about the way the brothers were with each other and with their guests—human, real, deeply serious about the things of God but with joy and humor, and thoroughly engaged with the everyday realities of life. The brother who had been celebrating the Eucharist would be seen next serving the dinner and then mopping the floor of the dining hall.

The young woman went home knowing that she had in some way to be part of this life. Over the next seven or eight years, with much prayer and questioning, she tried various possibilities. She became a Companion of this particular group of Franciscans, committed to supporting them in prayer and giving. It was good, but not enough.

Next, she explored the life of the sisters who followed Clare, living an enclosed life of contemplation near Oxford. She even resigned from her job and spent ten days with them as a postulant, one who was beginning to live the life—but soon realized that this was not for her. Returning to her career as a librarian, she then tested out the Third Order, those Franciscans who stayed in their own homes and jobs but committed to living in the Franciscan spirit and with an accountability to each other and to their rule of life. Nearly three years went by and all was going well. But just before she was due to apply to make her life commitment, God turned everything upside down again. She knew that this was not her way, and so withdrew before making her final commitment.

Finally, nearly ten years after that initial visit, she became a novice in the Community of St. Francis, the sisters' equivalent of the brothers she had first met, living in community, under vows of poverty, chastity, and obedience and engaging actively with the world.

Of course, that was only the beginning of more searching—was this the right way? Would they have her anyway? It was another eight years before she made her life vows, a final commitment to this particular part of the Franciscan family, and to this particular way of living the gospel in the footsteps of Francis and Clare.

Well, that's part of my story. It's not unusual. All over the world and in many of the churches, people are still discovering that the Franciscan way is their way of living the gospel.

But how did this way become an option for a twentieth-century British woman? It is a long way, in both time and space, from twelfth-century Catholic Italy to twentieth-century Anglican Britain.

In fact, the first Franciscans arrived in Britain in 1224, while Francis was still alive. Nine brothers, three of whom were English, arrived in Dover. Settling first in Canterbury, they soon had houses in London and Oxford. Between 1225 and 1230 they founded at least twelve more houses; by 1255 there were forty-nine houses and 1,242 friars. By this time there was also one house for women, and others followed.

The Reformation brought an end to the Franciscan religious life as it did to the monastic one. About six hundred friars had to leave their friaries and make their own way in the world. Only one small group of women moved to a country house and sought to continue to keep the Rule. But people continued to join the Franciscans, though they had to go abroad to do so. Some returned to England to work in a semisecret way, facing persecution at some times and more tolerance at others. Two groups of sisters, from Gravelines and Bruges, fled to England during the French Revolution and became established in that country. As tolerance for Catholics increased during the nineteenth century, friars too returned openly, and from mid-century new houses were established, to run parishes and engage in mission work. More houses of Poor Clares and of active Franciscan sisters were also founded.

All this renewed activity must have contributed to an increased interest in Francis and Franciscanism, which by the end of the century was also influencing the Anglican Church. The first Anglican Franciscan community was founded in 1894; it, together with other small communities of men, came together in the 1930s to form the Society of St. Francis (SSF). The contemplative life for women was established in 1950, and the active Community of St. Francis, founded in 1905, became part of SSF in the 1960s.

This lightning tour of the Franciscan life in one corner of the world shows one small part of the working out of the call to mission that is an important part of the Franciscan calling. Francis was the first founder of a religious community to provide specifically for mission, fulfilling in a literal way the great commission of Jesus, "Go therefore and make disciples of all nations" (Matthew 28:19). His brothers, unconfined to monasteries, could and did preach the gospel wherever they went. Europe was, of course, largely Christian already, but heresies abounded, and many were probably only nominally believers. There was much scope for rekindling the fires of devotion and calling those who had fallen away to repentance and return. But Francis also specifically wished that some of his brothers would go to "the Saracens"—that is, the Muslims—and other nonbelievers. His desire was that all the world should come to know and to praise God. In a letter to the brothers in charge of particular regions of the brotherhood, he exhorted, "And you must announce and preach [God's] praise to all peoples in such a manner that at every hour and whenever the bells are rung, praise, glory and honor are given to the all-powerful God throughout all the earth."[121]

The early life of the brothers reflected this missionary imperative and echoed the lifestyle described in Acts. Paul and the other early apostles traveled often in twos or threes, spending time in particular areas before reporting back to each other and to the church leaders. In a similar way, the early friars spent most of their time in pairs on the road. Once or twice a year, they returned to Assisi for a chapter meeting, where they would listen to Francis, share what had happened to them, and then be sent off again to preach the gospel.

This preaching was not to be only in words. Francis identified two ways of mission in his Earlier Rule—that of witness and that of proclamation. "All the brothers," he writes, "should preach by their deeds."[122] And he spells out what kind of deeds he means: "Not to engage in arguments or disputes, but to be subject to every human creature for God's sake (1 Peter 2:13) and to acknowledge that they are Christians."[123] Working in pairs gave the brothers a daily opportunity to demonstrate what being a Christian meant, in the way that they related to each other. Their preaching had to be backed up by their lives, lives that were transparent to those among whom they worked. In the early days they had no houses of their own, but lived wherever they could find shelter. They took as their model Jesus' words when he sent out his disciples: "Whatever town or village you enter, find out who in it is worthy, and stay there until you leave" (Matthew 10:11).

Sometimes this witness of life was sufficient to arouse the curiosity of others. Brother Bernard was sent by Francis to Bologna. His strange and tattered habit earned him many insults, and the children threw stones and dust at him. But he bore all this not only patiently but joyfully, and continued to go out daily into the marketplace. Finally a lawyer, convinced of Bernard's holiness by his behavior, approached him and asked, "Who are you, and why have you come here?" Then Bernard gave him the Rule of St. Francis to read. The lawyer was so impressed by what he read that he gave Bernard a house to use as a friary.

"Another way," writes Francis, "is to proclaim the word of God when they see that it pleases the Lord."[124] As Jesus sometimes simply went about doing the work of God but at other times set out to teach and to preach the kingdom, so Francis himself and the early friars not only acted but also spoke. When they went to Pope Innocent III to seek approval of their First Rule, they also received permission "to preach penance to all."[125] This permission was important. In the medieval church, permission to preach was confined to bishops and priests, and most of the early brothers were laymen.

Perhaps it was to reassure the church authorities of the orthodoxy of their preaching that Francis set out a model sermon in his Earlier Rule, Chapter XXI. Simple and easily memorized, it begins in praise and moves on to penance. But some needed no model for their preaching, including Francis himself. As Celano writes,

> For when he so very often preached the word of God to thousands of people, he was as sure of himself as though he were speaking with a familiar companion. He looked upon the greatest multitude of people as one person, and he preached to one as he would to a multitude. Out of the purity of his mind he provided for himself security in preaching a sermon, and without thinking about it beforehand, he spoke wonderful things to all and things not heard before.[126]

Celano goes on to relate that sometimes Francis did plan beforehand what he would say, but then forgot it when the time came. He would confess to his hearers that all that he had prepared had gone out of his mind, but then would speak with great eloquence. But if he had nothing to say, he would simply bless the people and this would satisfy them.

Francis seems to have preached with his whole being. Once, before Pope Honorius and the cardinals, he spoke with such fervor that "he moved his feet as though he were dancing."[127] His preaching drew great crowds of men and women, priests and religious. "Every age and every sex hurried to see the wonderful things that the Lord was newly working in the world through his servant."[128] He preached not only to all people, but to all creation.

The most famous story is of his preaching to the birds, near Bevagna, where he came across a large flock of them as he traveled. He greeted them and, when they did not fly away, spoke to them, reminding them of all that God had given them and calling on them to praise their Creator. Then he blessed them and made the sign of the cross over them, after which they flew away. Bonaventure tells this story, not in a chapter about Francis' love of animals, but in one entitled "The Efficacy of Francis' Preaching," and in the same chapter indicates how witness and proclamation came together in Francis. "Francis," he writes, "had first convinced himself of the truth of what he preached to others by practicing it in his own life, and so he proclaimed the truth confidently, without fear of reproof."[129]

Francis was not the only powerful preacher among the brothers. Antony of Padua, a younger contemporary of Francis, was preaching before the pope and cardinals, men from many different nations and languages. He spoke so well that each understood him as perfectly as though Antony had spoken in their own language, and echoing the puzzlement of the crowd on the day of Pentecost, they asked each other, "Doesn't this man who is preaching come from Spain? How is it that we each hear him in our own language?"[130]

Such preaching undoubtedly contributed to the rapid spread of the brothers. They were highly visible, preaching often outside in public places rather than inside churches. They preached a simple message that called for response, and for many the response was to join them. The growing community could spread their message more widely, and from 1217 brothers began to go outside Italy to countries north of the Alps, and across the Mediterranean to North Africa and the Holy Land.

It was from Assisi that the brothers set off, commissioned by Francis at their chapter meetings, and it was often to Assisi that they returned, to report on their endeavors. They reported not only to their brothers but also to Clare and her sisters at San Damiano. The sisters' sense of sharing in Francis' mission was sharpened by the regular flow of visitors and news, and their prayers and concern supported the brothers as they went out, often into isolated or sometimes dangerous places. Despite their life of enclosure, the sisters were deeply involved in mission. Women inspired by the preaching of the brothers looked to San Damiano for a model of how they might live the Franciscan life, so that by the time of Clare's death more than 150 communities counted themselves as belonging to her form of life. Sometimes these had been founded by sisters sent out from San Damiano: For example, five sisters went to Prague in 1234 to join Agnes in her new foundation, but many had sprung up independently, perhaps after some correspondence with Clare.

In the Rule imposed on the sisters by Cardinal Hugolino around 1218, founding a new monastery was the only legitimate reason for a sister to leave the enclosure of the monastery she had joined. His model of enclosure took its shape from the responsibility of a father of the time to protect the virginity of his daughters until they were given to their husband. As the sisters usually lived in or near the city, this protection had to be physical in the form of walls and grilles. The sisters were not to be seen by, or to see, those outside. In addition, perpetual silence was to be kept.

When Clare wrote her Rule, she kept the fundamental restrictions, but the spirit of enclosure was somewhat different. She allowed that a sister may leave the monastery "for some useful, reasonable, evident, and approved purpose."[131] As we saw in Chapter 3, Clare herself left San Damiano to eat with Francis at St. Mary of the Angels. When the sisters talked to a visitor in the parlor, they might draw back the curtain from the grille that separated them. Complete silence was to be kept at all times in the church, the dormitory, and the dining area, but only at night in the rest of the monastery. Where Hugolino's rule legislated for a life of penitential confinement, Clare's provided for a necessary withdrawal in order to focus life on the essentials. The Bull of Clare's canonization captures very poetically the paradox of the enclosed life—the light that is kept confined and limited shines more brightly:

> Hidden within, [Clare] extended herself abroad. In fact, Clare was hidden, yet her life was visible. Clare

was silent, yet her reputation became widespread. She was kept hidden in a cell, but was known throughout the world. It should not be surprising that a light so enkindled, so illuminating, could not be kept from shining brilliantly and giving clear light in the house of the Lord.[132]

Her attitude to enclosure is shown by the fact that at one time Clare considered leaving the monastery to go to Morocco, where, on January 16, 1220, five friars—Berard, Peter, Accursion, Adiuto, and Ottone—had been martyred, the first in the order. Clare too wanted to offer herself for martyrdom, which she saw as the ultimate gift of the self to God. Sister Balvina, one of the witnesses at Clare's canonization, remembered that she "had such a fervent spirit that she would have willingly endured martyrdom for the defense of the faith and her order for the love of God. Before she was sick, she desired to go to those parts of Morocco where it was said the brothers had suffered martyrdom."[133]

Francis' love for God was equally great, so that he too was willing to risk martyrdom to spread the gospel. He made several attempts to go "to the Saracens." A voyage to Syria in 1212 ended in shipwreck in Dalmatia; an attempt to reach Morocco a year or two later was ended by illness in Spain. But in 1219, during the Fifth Crusade, Francis traveled to Damietta, on the Nile delta, where he met and tried to convert the sultan of Egypt. Hostility between Christians and Muslims was such that even attempting to reach the sultan put Francis in danger of death. But, though captured and beaten by the soldiers, he remained steadfast, preaching the gospel in word and by example, and refusing the gifts that the Sultan offered because of his commitment to poverty. The Sultan seems to have been impressed, listening to him often, and allowing Francis and his companions to preach wherever they wanted. But he could not convert for fear of a revolt among his people, and finally Francis and his companions left and returned home. This encounter has become for many, especially for Franciscans, a model of inter-faith relations that are honest about differences, but respectful of each other's commitment.

While many who heard Francis and his brothers preach were willing and able to leave their homes to follow him, whether as friars on the road or sisters in the monastery, there were others whose existing commitments made that impossible. Francis had a concern for them too. As Jesus called some who he met to leave all and follow him but sent others back to their homes to spread the message there (Luke 18:18-23; Mark 5:19; Matthew 9:7), so Francis wanted to make it possible for all people to follow Christ. The story is told of his preaching at a village called Savurniano, and making such an impact that the entire village wanted to follow him, leaving the village abandoned. But he dissuaded them, telling them instead that they could live the life of the gospel where they were. This was the beginning of the Third Order.

Celano tells that Francis gave these followers a norm of life, as he had done for his own brothers and for Clare and her sisters. Although the earliest form has not survived, the first version of the "Letter to the Faithful" is thought to contain it. It is a challenging call to a life of penance, based on a deep love of God and a growing relationship to him as Father, Spouse, and Brother. The Brothers and Sisters of Penance, as they were called at first, were a real force for renewal in the church of the time. They took a radical stance, refusing to bear arms or take oaths, which placed them on the margins of their society. They sought to serve others, as Francis did, in very practical ways.

Countess Elizabeth of Thuringia, for example, founded a hospital for the poor in 1223 and worked in it herself—unheard-of for a member of the nobility. Luchesio Modestini, a contemporary of Francis, another merchant's son, sold his business and served in the local hospital at Poggibonsi. His special ministry was to travel down to the plains to collect the old and helpless who had contracted fevers and malaria. Then he brought them, on his donkey, or even carried on his back, up to the fresh air of his town, and to the hospital where they could be cared for.

Finally, there were those called to follow more particularly the way of solitude and prayer, which was a part of Francis' own call. He had lived in this way in the early days of his conversion, seeking out lonely places in which to pray. But his call to preach the gospel was too strong for him to remain permanently in this way of life. He recognized it, however, as a genuine call, and later in life wrote a Rule for "those who wish to live religiously in hermitages."[134] Characteristically, it combines provision for an intense life of prayer with a commitment to the life of brotherhood that was so important as a witness to the gospel. The brothers in hermitages were to live in small groups of three or four; at any time, two were to be "mothers," taking care of the practical details of life, while the others were to be "sons," free to give themselves entirely to prayer. From time to time they were to exchange roles. Flexibility and realism are the hallmarks of this Rule.

Active brothers preaching the word by witness, proclamation, and martyrdom, contemplative sisters upholding the world in prayer, lay people combining their secular life with a radical commitment to Christ, hermits focusing more deeply on prayer in solitude or small groups—all these ways of being Franciscan were called into being by Francis himself, and all are still alive and active in the twenty-first century. Since his time, women too have developed ways of living the active Franciscan life, and some members of the Third Order have chosen to live in community.

In the Franciscan life down the centuries and across the world can be seen reflected Paul's image of the body with many members—each with its own role, each contributing to the whole (1 Corinthians 12:12-27).

But Francis also draws those outside the church, those who would not call themselves Christians. It is no coincidence that when, in October 1986, Pope John Paul II called a meeting of leaders of all religions to pray for peace, he chose Assisi as their meeting place. The ecological movement has found much inspiration in Francis' love of creation, in his vision of all of creation as brother and sister. Francis' radical commitment to poverty has inspired others to value its gifts as they seek to live alongside the poor of the world.

His own vision encompassed all of this. In his Earlier Rule he lists all the people he can think of—all the ranks of the church and of society, and concludes with "all the small and the great, all peoples, races, tribes, and tongues, all nations and all peoples everywhere on earth, who are and who will be"[135]—in other words, everyone, everywhere, in every time, calling them all to faith, to penance, and hence to salvation.

It is this universal vision that makes Francis a saint for everyone, and that makes the Franciscan project such an exciting and life-giving one. God called Francis and Clare to be a particular gift to the church and the world, to incarnate one particular way of following Christ. But the gift, and the way, are not simply for the past, not only something to which we can look back, or even something that we simply try to imitate. As a present-day Poor Clare puts it, "Because they were called by the living God, they are the point of departure for a gift which is developing."[136]

Or, as Francis put it, "I have done what was mine to do; may Christ teach you what you are to do."[137] ❧

Notes

1. Bonaventure, "Major Life of St. Francis," 3:1, *St. Francis of Assisi: Writings and Early Biographies, English Omnibus of the Sources for the Life of St. Francis,* 3rd rev. ed., ed. Marion A. Habig (Chicago: Society for Promoting Chirstian Knowledge, 1979), 646.

2. Thomas of Celano, "The First Life of St. Francis," 83, in Habig, *English Omnibus,* 298.

3. The Testament, 14, in *Francis and Clare: The Complete Works,* ed. Regis J. Armstrong and Ignatius Brady (New York: Paulist Press, 1982), 15.

4. The Earlier Rule, Prologue, 2, in Armstrong and Brady, *Francis and Clare,* 108.

5. The Later Rule, I:1, in Armstrong and Brady, *Francis and Clare,* 137.

6. The Testament, 16, in Armstrong and Brady, *Francis and Clare,* 155.

7. The Admonitions, 7, in Armstrong and Brady, *Francis and Clare,* 30.

8. Regis J. Armstrong, *St. Francis of Assisi: Writings for a Gospel Life* (Slough, U.K.: St. Paul's, 1994), 97.

9. The First Version of the Letter to the Faithful, 21, in Armstrong and Brady, *Francis and Clare,* 65.

10. Richard Rohr, *Simplicity: The Art of Living* (New York: Crossroad Publishing, 1995), 113.

11. The Testament, 14, in Armstrong and Brady, *Francis and Clare,* 154.

12. "The Legend of St. Clare," 12, in *Clare of Assisi: Early Documents*, ed. Regis J. Armstrong (New York: Paulist Press, 1988), 202.

13. The Testament, 27–28, in Armstrong and Brady, *Francis and Clare,* 155.

14. Thomas of Celano, "The First Life," 115, in Habig, *English Omnibus,* 329.

15. Bonaventure, "Major Life," X:6, in Habig, *English Omnibus,* 710.

16. The First Letter to Blessed Agnes of Prague, 9–10, in Armstrong and Brady, *Francis and Clare,* 191.

17. Thomas of Celano, "The First Life," 86, in Habig, *English Omnibus,* 301.

18. Ugolino, *The Little Flowers of St. Francis of Assisi,* 14 (London: H. R. Allenson, n.d.), 199.

19. The Fourth Letter to Blessed Agnes of Prague, 23, in Armstrong and Brady, *Francis and Clare,* 205.

20. A Letter to the Entire Order, 27, in Armstrong and Brady, *Francis and Clare,* 58.

21. A Letter to the Entire Order, 27, in Armstrong and Brady, *Francis and Clare,* 56.

22. A Letter to the Clergy, 12, in Armstrong and Brady, *Francis and Clare,* 50.

23. "The Legend of St. Clare," 37, in Armstrong, *Clare of Assisi,* 224.

24. Bonaventure, "Major Life," I:1, in Habig, *English Omnibus,* 635.

25. Glossa Ordinaria, quoted in Theophile Desbonnets, "The Franciscan Reading of the Scriptures," in *Francis of Assisi Today,* ed. Christian Duquoc and Casiano Floristan (New York: T&T Clark/Seabury, 1981), 42.

26. Marie Beha, "Praying with Clare of Assisi," *The Cord* 47, no. 4 (1997): 185.

27. Acts of the Process of Canonization, 4:4, in Armstrong, *Clare of Assisi,* 146.

28. Acts of the Process of Canonization, 2:17, in Armstrong, *Clare of Assisi,* 137–138.

29. Acts of the Process of Canonization, 1:9, in Armstrong, *Clare of Assisi,* 131.

30. Acts of the Process of Canonization, 3:7, in Armstrong, *Clare of Assisi,* 140.

31. Acts of the Process of Canonization, 3:18, in Armstrong, *Clare of Assisi,* 142.

32. Thomas of Celano, "The First Life," 71, in Habig, *English Omnibus,* 288.

33. Society of Saint Francis, *Celebrating Common Prayer: A Version of the Daily Office SSF* (London: Mowbray, 1992), 8.

34. Society of Saint Francis, *The Daily Office SSF,* 287.

35. The Prayer Before the Crucifix, in Armstrong and Brady, *Francis and Clare*, 103.

36. Society of Saint Francis, *The Daily Office SSF*, 290.

37. Society of Saint Francis, *The Daily Office SSF*, 288.

38. Society of Saint Francis, *The Daily Office SSF*, 289.

39. Society of Saint Francis, *The Daily Office SSF*, 289.

40. The Rule of Saint Clare, VII:2, in Armstrong and Brady, *Francis and Clare*, 219.

41. The Letter to Ermentrude of Bruges, 11, in Armstrong and Brady, *Francis and Clare*, 208.

42. Frances Teresa Downing, "Clare of Assisi and the Tradition of Spiritual Guidance," *The Cord* 48, no. 4 (1998): 163.

43. Downing, "Clare of Assisi and the Tradition of Spiritual Guidance," 166.

44. Downing, "Clare of Assisi and the Tradition of Spiritual Guidance," 166.

45. Downing, "Clare of Assisi and the Tradition of Spiritual Guidance," 163.

46. The Third Letter to Blessed Agnes of Prague, 13, in Armstrong and Brady, *Francis and Clare*, 200.

47. The Fourth Letter to Blessed Agnes of Prague, 14, in Armstrong and Brady, *Francis and Clare*, 204.

48. The Fourth Letter to Blessed Agnes of Prague, 17, in Armstrong and Brady, *Francis and Clare*, 204.

49. The Fourth Letter to Blessed Agnes of Prague, 24, in Armstrong and Brady, *Francis and Clare*, 205.

50. The Testament of Saint Clare, 6, in Armstrong and Brady, *Francis and Clare*, 228.

51. The Testament of Saint Clare, 6, in Armstrong and Brady, *Francis and Clare*, 228.

52. The First Version of the Letter to the Faithful, 7–10, in Armstrong and Brady, *Francis and Clare*, 63.

53. The Rule of Saint Clare, II:11, in Armstrong and Brady, *Francis and Clare*, 213.

54. The Earlier Rule, III:13, in Armstrong and Brady, *Francis and Clare*, 112.

55. A Letter to Brother Leo, 3, in Armstrong and Brady, *Francis and Clare*, 48.

56. Thomas of Celano, "The Second Life of St. Francis," 214, in Habig, *English Omnibus*, 534.

57. The Later Rule, X:8, and The Rule of Saint Clare, X:7, in Armstrong and Brady, *Francis and Clare*, 144, 222.

58. Thomas of Celano, "The Second Life," 95, in Habig, *English Omnibus*, 441.

59. The Later Rule, V:2, in Armstrong and Brady, *Francis and Clare*, 140.

60. The Office of the Passion, Antiphon, 2, in Armstrong and Brady, *Francis and Clare*, 82.

61. The Salutation of the Blessed Virgin Mary, 1, in Armstrong and Brady, *Francis and Clare*, 149.

62. The Form of Life Given to Saint Clare and Her Sisters, 1, in Armstrong and Brady, *Francis and Clare*, 45.

63. Bonaventure, "Major Life," IX:1, in Habig, *English Omnibus*, 698.

64. The First Version of the Letter to the Faithful, 11–13, in Armstrong and Brady, *Francis and Clare*, 63.

65. The First Letter to Blessed Agnes of Prague, 12, in Armstrong and Brady, *Francis and Clare*, 191.

66. The First Letter to Blessed Agnes of Prague, 5–7, in Armstrong and Brady, *Francis and Clare*, 190–191.

67. The Rule of Saint Clare, X:3, in Armstrong and Brady, *Francis and Clare*, 222.

68. The Earlier Rule, VI:3–4, in Armstrong and Brady, *Francis and Clare*, 114.

69. The Later Rule, VI:7, in Armstrong and Brady, *Francis and Clare*, 141.

70. The Rule of Saint Clare, X:4, in Armstrong and Brady, *Francis and Clare*, 222.

71. The Rule of Saint Clare, X:5, in Armstrong and Brady, *Francis and Clare*, 222.

72. The Rule of Saint Clare, VIII:9, in Armstrong and Brady, *Francis and Clare*, 220.

73. The Earlier Rule, X:1, in Armstrong and Brady, *Francis and Clare*, 118.

74. The Form of Life Given to Saint Clare and Her Sisters, in Armstrong and Brady, *Francis and Clare*, 44–45.

75. The Earlier Rule, XII:1, in Armstrong and Brady, *Francis and Clare*, 119.

76. Seamus Mulholland, "St. Francis and the Themes of Medieval Literature," *The Cord* 44, no. 4 (1994): 116–117.

77. Society of Saint Francis, *The Daily Office SSF*, 232–33.

78. Thomas of Celano, "The Second Life," 9, in Habig, *English Omnibus*, 369.

79. Murray Bodo, *The Way of St. Francis: The Challenge of Franciscan Spirituality for Everyone* (Cincinnati, OH: St. Anthony Messenger Press, 1995), 70.

80. The Testament, 1–3, in Armstrong and Brady, *Francis and Clare*, 154.

81. The First Version of the Letter to the Faithful, 2:11; compare The Second Version of the Letter to the Faithful, 69, in Armstrong and Brady, *Francis and Clare*, 64, 72.

82. The Second Version of the Letter to the Faithful, in Armstrong and Brady, *Francis and Clare*, 68.

83. Thomas of Celano, "The First Life," 94, in Habig, *English Omnibus*, 309.

84. Thomas of Celano, "The First Life," 115, in Habig, *English Omnibus*, 329.

85. Thomas of Celano, "The First Life," 95, in Habig, *English Omnibus*, 310.

86. Thomas of Celano, "The Second Life," 135, in Habig, *English Omnibus*, 472.

87. Bonaventure, "Minor Life of St. Francis," 6:2, in Habig, *English Omnibus*, 822.

88. Bonaventure, "Major Life," 13:10, in Habig, *English Omnibus*, 735–36.

89. "Legend of the Three Companions," 14, in Habig, *English Omnibus*, 904.

90. Armstrong, *St. Francis of Assisi*, 183.

91. Acts of the Process of Canonization, 11:2, in Armstrong, *Clare of Assisi*, 162.

92. Marco Bartoli, *Clare of Assisi* (London: Darton, Longman & Todd, 1993), 37.

93. The Testament, 1, in Armstrong and Brady, *Francis and Clare*, 154.

94. The Earlier Rule, XXI:7, in Armstrong and Brady, *Francis and Clare*, 126.

95. The Earlier Rule, XXI:9, in Armstrong and Brady, *Francis and Clare*, 126.

96. The First Version of the Letter to the Faithful, 1:5–6, in Armstrong and Brady, *Francis and Clare*, 63.

97. Bodo, *The Way of St. Francis*, 11–12.

98. A Letter to a Minister, 3, in Armstrong and Brady, *Francis and Clare*, 75.

99. A Letter to a Minister, 9–10, in Armstrong and Brady, *Francis and Clare*, 75.

100. A Letter to a Minister, 11, in Armstrong and Brady, *Francis and Clare*, 75.

101. Acts of the Process of Canonization, 3:20, in Armstrong, *Clare of Assisi*, 143.

102. Thomas of Celano, "The Second Life," 217, in Habig, *English Omnibus*, 536.

103. The Last Will Written for Saint Clare and Her Sisters, 1–2, in Armstrong and Brady, *Francis and Clare*, 46.

104. The Testament of Saint Clare, 10, in Armstrong and Brady, *Francis and Clare*, 229.

105. The Testament of Saint Clare, 13, in Armstrong and Brady, *Francis and Clare*, 230.

106. The Second Version of the Letter to the Faithful, 5, in Armstrong and Brady, *Francis and Clare*, 67.

107. "Legend of the Three Companions," 7, in Habig, *English Omnibus*, 896.

108. Thomas of Celano, "The Second Life," 55, in Habig, *English Omnibus*, 410–11.

109. Bonaventure, "Major Life," VIII:5, in Habig, *English Omnibus*, 691.

110. Bonaventure, "Major Life," VIII:5, in Habig, *English Omnibus*, 692.

111. The Admonitions, 6:3, in Armstrong and Brady, *Francis and Clare*, 29.

112. The Admonitions, 2:3, in Armstrong and Brady, *Francis and Clare*, 27.

113. The Earlier Rule, XVII:7, in Armstrong and Brady, *Francis and Clare*, 123.

114. The First Letter to Blessed Agnes of Prague, 30, in Armstrong and Brady, *Francis and Clare*, 193.

115. Sacrum Commercium, 25, in Habig, *English Omnibus*, 1566.

116. H. A. Williams, *Poverty, Chastity and Obedience* (London: Mitchell Beazley, 1975), 40.

117. The Admonitions, 27:3, in Armstrong and Brady, *Francis and Clare*, 35.

118. The Earlier Rule, VII:16, in Armstrong and Brady, *Francis and Clare*, 115–16.

119. The Rule of Saint Clare, VIII:1, in Armstrong and Brady, *Francis and Clare*, 219–20.

120. The Earlier Rule, VII:8, in Armstrong and Brady, *Francis and Clare*, 115.

121. The First Letter to the Custodians, 8, in Armstrong and Brady, *Francis and Clare*, 53.

122. The Earlier Rule, XVII:3, in Armstrong and Brady, *Francis and Clare*, 122.

123. The Earlier Rule, XVI:6, in Armstrong and Brady, *Francis and Clare*, 121.

124. The Earlier Rule, XVI:7, in Armstrong and Brady, *Francis and Clare,* 121.

125. "Legend of the Three Companions," 51, in Habig, *English Omnibus,* 937.

126. Thomas of Celano, "The First Life," 72, in Habig, *English Omnibus,* 289.

127. Thomas of Celano, "The First Life," 73, in Habig, *English Omnibus,* 290.

128. Thomas of Celano, "The First Life," 36, in Habig, *English Omnibus,* 259.

129. Bonaventure, "Major Life," XII:8, in Habig, *English Omnibus,* 725.

130. Ugolino, *The Little Flowers,* 38, 185.

131. The Rule of Saint Clare, II:7, in Armstrong and Brady, *Francis and Clare,* 212.

132. The Bull of Canonization, 3, 4, in Armstrong, *Clare of Assisi,* 177–78.

133. Acts of the Process of Canonization, 7:2, in Armstrong, *Clare of Assisi,* 153–54.

134. The Rule for Hermitages, 1, in Armstrong and Brady, *Francis and Clare,* 147.

135. The Earlier Rule, XXIII:7, in Armstrong and Brady, *Francis and Clare,* 132.

136. Frances Teresa Downing, "Clare of Assisi: A Woman for Today," *The Cord* 46, no. 4 (1996): 10.

137. Thomas of Celano, "The Second Life," 214, in Habig, *English Omnibus,* 534.

Bibliography and Further Reading

Armstrong, Regis J. *Clare of Assisi: Early Documents*. New York: Paulist Press, 1988.

Armstrong, Regis J. *St. Francis of Assisi: Writings for a Gospel Life*. Slough: St. Paul's, 1994.

Armstrong, Regis J., and Ignatius C. Brady. *Francis and Clare: The Complete Works*. New York: Paulist Press, 1982.

Armstrong, Regis J., J. A. Wayne Hellmann, and William J. Short. *Francis of Assisi, Early Documents: The Saint; The Founder; The Prophet*. Hyde Park, NY: New City Press, 1999–2001.

Bartoli, Marco. *Clare of Assisi*. London: Darton, Longman & Todd, 1993.

Bodo, Murray. *Clare, a Light in the Garden*. Cincinnati, OH: St. Anthony Messenger Press, 1979.

Bodo, Murray. *Francis, the Journey and the Dream*. Cincinnati, OH: St. Anthony Messenger Press, 1972.

Bodo, Murray. *The Way of St. Francis: The Challenge of Franciscan Spirituality for Everyone*. Cincinnati, OH: St. Anthony Messenger Press, 1995.

Bonaventure. *The Soul's Journey Into God; The Tree of Life; The Life of St. Francis*. Translated by Ewert Cousins. New York: Paulist Press, 1978.

Coelho, Christopher. *A New Kind of Fool: Meditations on St. Francis*. London: Burns and Oates, 1991.

Doyle, Eric. *St. Francis and the Song of Brotherhood and Sisterhood*. St. Bonaventure, NY: Franciscan Institute, 1980.

Dunstan, Peta. *This Poor Sort: A History of the European Province of the Society of St. Francis*. London: Darton, Longman & Todd, 1997.

Duquoc, Christian, and Casiano Floristan, eds. *Francis of Assisi Today*. New York: T&T Clark/Seabury, 1981.

Frances Teresa, OSC. *Living the Incarnation: Praying with Francis and Clare of Assisi*. London: Darton, Longman & Todd, 1993.

Frances Teresa, OSC. *This Living Mirror: Reflections on Clare of Assisi*. London: Darton, Longman & Todd, 1995.

Frugoni, Chiara. *Francis of Assisi*. London: SCM Press, 1998.

Habig, Marion A., ed., *St. Francis of Assisi: Writings and Early Biographies*. English Omnibus of the Sources for the Life of St. Francis, 3rd rev. ed. London: Society for Promoting Christian Knowledge, 1979.

Ramon, Brother. *Franciscan Spirituality: Following St. Francis Today*. London: Society for Promoting Christian Knowledge, 1994.

Robson, Michael. *St. Francis of Assisi: The Legend and the Life*. London: Geoffrey Chapman, 1997.

Short, William. *Poverty and Joy: The Franciscan Tradition*. London: Darton, Longman & Todd, 1999.

Society of Saint Francis. *Celebrating Common Prayer: A Version of the Daily Office SSF*. London: Mowbray, 1992.

Stoutzenberger, Joseph M., and John D. Bohrer. *Praying with St. Francis*. Winona, MN: St. Mary's Press, 1989.